Guitars

Guitars

A Celebration of Pure Mojo

By David Schiller

WORKMAN PUBLISHING • NEW YORK

Library of Congress Cataloging-in-Publication Data is available.

ISBN-13: 978-0-7611-3800-6

Workman books are available at special discounts when purchased in bulk for
premiums and sales promotions as well as for fund-raising or educational use.
Special editions or book excerpts can also be created to specification. For details,
contact the Special Sales Director at the address below.

Art direction: Janet Vicario
Layout design: Ellen Nygaard
Front cover guitar: Gibson

WORKMAN PUBLISHING COMPANY, INC.
225 Varick Street
New York, NY 10014-4381
www.workman.com

Printed in China

First printing April 2008
10 9 8 7 6 5 4 3 2 1

For The Seven Studs,
the world's greatest band

CONTENTS

Martin 0-18T, 1950

Ibanez Jem, 1980s

*Ribbecke green archtop,
1995*

THE 6-STRING SPELL

There has never been another musical instrument like the guitar. There's never been an instrument as versatile: It plays rhythm, it plays melody (sometimes endlessly, when it's called "lead"), and it is as sophisticated harmonically as a piano. In the hands of a highly skilled player, in fact, it can perform all of these roles simultaneously. It is arguably the world's most pleasing solo instrument—try sitting in the park with a tuba—and also performs brilliantly as accompaniment, particularly in the age of amplification. The guitar loves the company of its siblings, whether in the classic two-guitar rock band configuration, or en masse, as in Glenn Branca's powerful symphony for 100 electric guitars. Its tonal

Epiphone Casino, 1965, that once belonged to Howlin' Wolf.

Bambina (Baby) Guitar, in case, 1870

palette is so far-ranging, aided by various construction techniques and goals, that there is not a genre or style of music to which it doesn't belong. It is essential to rock, blues, country, folk, reggae, R&B, funk, and just about every other popular style, but it has also played a starring role in jazz, has accrued a centuries-long reputation as a classical instrument, is the soul of flamenco, is sampled and featured in rap, is used in the gospel mix, and has even appeared in opera—well, rock operas *Tommy* and *Hair*, to name a couple.

The guitar is also the most democratic of instruments, and this begins to get at the core of its appeal. Throughout the centuries of its evolution, the guitar suffered a seesaw

Domino Baron, 1967

reputation, swinging between high and low culture,
falling into and out of favor with the elite. But, no
matter which royal court was having its brief love
affair with it, the guitar never lost its street credibility.
There has never been an instrument quite as easy to play,
though so difficult to master. A beginner—yes, you, even if you've never
strummed a single note—can pick up a guitar, and within a few hours play
a handful of songs, within weeks entertain the family at the holidays, and within
months form a rock band and hit the highway. Everyone is welcome to the guitar.
Whole reputations have been made by using the simplest of musical constructions—
open chords, the basic triads like C, D , and G—in the simplest of pop forms, the
I—IV—V progression. Yet, whether one is self-taught (in keeping with its democratic
status, the guitar seems to attract a lot of autodidacts, and how often have you heard

Maccaferri New Romancer, 1950s

of a self-taught cellist?) or conservatory-trained, the guitar defies finitude. The complexity of the fretboard alone, factored by alternate tunings, makes learning all the guitar has to offer impossible.

Affordability and accessibility help keep the guitar democratic, which raises one of the many paradoxes surrounding the instrument. A fairly predictable correlation exists between price and quality, particularly with acoustic guitars. More money means better quality wood and workmanship, and that generally, though certainly not always, translates into a better sounding, better playing instrument. But even the cheapest guitar can possess mojo. And despite the fact that the highest of high-end guitars is handmade, some of the best-sounding guitars ever created came off the factory floor. So no matter what, just about anybody who wants a guitar can afford one.

Though its history reaches back 500 years, the guitar really came into its own in the early part of the 20th century, shepherded along by a few key builders, innovators, and musicians. The guitar grew louder. It grew softer. It growled. It keened. It chunked, and thrummed, and the music, just like the instrument, developed exponentially. By the midcentury mark, the guitar was everywhere, at dances and in dorm rooms, in the park or at the concert hall, on the radio or on television. There were guitar groups and guitar poets and guitar heroes, and from the image of the hipster troubadour created by Bob Dylan to the otherworldly experience of Jimi Hendrix weaving massive, charismatic solos out of thin air, the guitar became, by the 1960s, the preferred tool for self-expression.

The guitar, particularly for men, who are not always good at self-expression, is a natural outlet, whether for a sensitive wordless sentiment or an aggressive heavy metal minor-key solo.

William Hall & Sons, c. 1850

It behaves, at times, like sports or cars. Put a group of guys together, mention
the word guitar, and about half of them either play or played or wish they had
time to play, used to be in a band or are in a band or want to form a band, and
are quick to compare guitars they own or owned, are buying, or are adding
to their wish list. Message boards on the Internet abound with discussions
about tone woods and fingernails vs. pick, and the effect of changing the
material of the bridge pins. And let's not forget the conquest factor.
A common acronym is G.A.S.—Guitar Acquisition Syndrome—the
feeling that you absolutely positively must have yet another guitar.
Players go to guitar stores basically to flirt, innocently cheating
on the Martin at home by spending a few hours playing the
Gibsons at the local Guitar Center. Players scheme about how
to slip another guitar into the house, whether selling one off
or waiting for a tax refund or pulling off a quid pro quo with

Gibson J-45, 1968

a spouse. So it should not be a surprise to learn that the neighbor in the modest colonial who drives a twelve-year-old car owns 21 guitars, having just bought the last one online for $4,000.

And why not have 21 guitars? The person who answers with "you can only play one at a time" shows a facile misreading of both instrument and player. Every guitar has its own voice. Every guitar plays differently, feels different in the hand, looks different. Pluck a string and the sound goes right into your body, and sometimes it's a sound that's impossible to live without. No matter what else happens in the day, to sit and play a few favorite chords or riffs is transporting. The guitar's body vibrates into your chest, and its song envelops your ears like a mist, time dissolves, and right there, all around you, is something unspeakably beautiful. Fingering mistakes don't matter; even the music is of secondary importance. It's pure tone, the pure experience

Hopf Saturn 63, c. 1965

of something eternal. Then throw in drums, a bass, and a few more guitar-playing friends, and the moment shifts to ecstasy.

Because guitars, even assembly-line solid-body electrics, are intimate and deeply personal once they become a part of the player, the history of the modern guitar is a riot of styles, colors, sizes, and shapes, all designed to build on that mystical connection between individual player and instrument. Each guitar seems to say play me, possess me, I'll make you the coolest guitarist around. Some guitars murmur with understated plainness, some wink with abalone and gold-plated tuning keys, and some shout with outlandish designs and graphics. And for other guitars, it's an association with an idol that

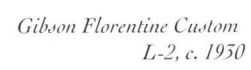

Gibson Florentine Custom
L-2, c. 1950

Detail of guitar by Jakob Ertel, Italy, c. 1690

works its charm: Pick up a B.B. King Lucille by Gibson, and the sweetest blues will issue forth from your fingers. Play Martin's gleaming black Johnny Cash D-35, and your music will have the stone-cold ring of truth.

GUITARS: A CELEBRATION OF PURE MOJO features approximately 500 guitars. Its aim is not to quantify, qualify, or analyze, nor does it try to speak for the scholar, social historian, or dyed-in-the-wool collector. This is a celebration of the instrument—famous instruments and forgotten instruments, milestone designs and dead-end experiments, ravishing beauties and instruments as bluntly functional as a hammer. It's a tribute to the pleasure, the quirky design, the spell that the guitar has cast over us. It's about joy, and ultimately, even if only fleetingly, soul. Just like the guitar itself.

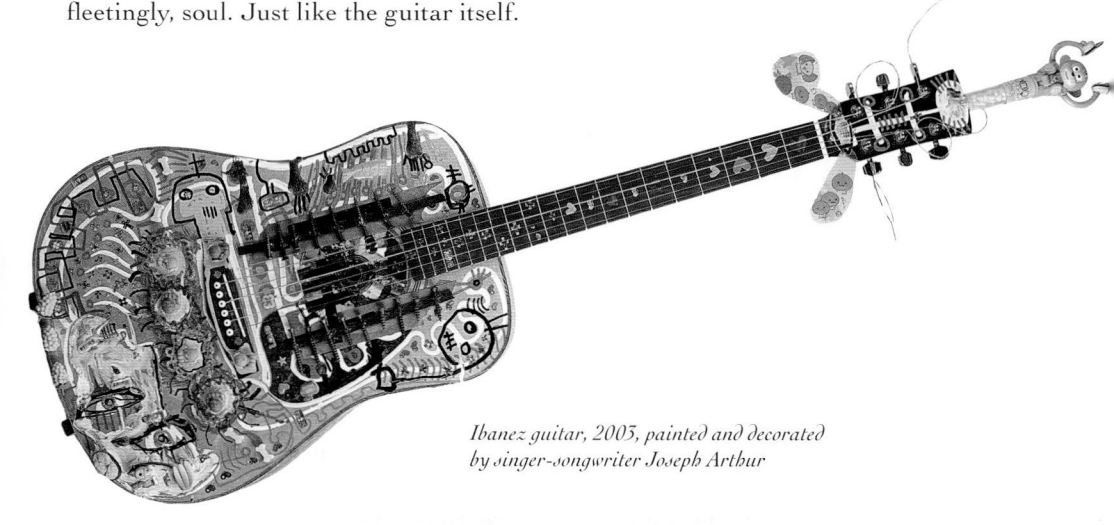

Ibanez guitar, 2003, painted and decorated by singer-songwriter Joseph Arthur

ONE

That Tone

*Gibson Everly Brothers,
1968*

WOOD, AIR, STRINGS—MAGIC

icture an early hunter, kicking back after the day's chase. He starts plucking the string of his bow. It produces a pleasant, even hypnotic sound. He plucks it higher on the string. The sound changes. Then lower on the string. Hmmmm, a different change. Plucks it, and hums along, makes a song. Pleased, he reaches for a slug of whatever fermented beverage is his clan's drink of choice, and then starts all over again. Voilà—the first "guitarist."

Then, in one of those leaps that seem both impossible and inevitable, another person, some tinkerer or a dreamer, or maybe an inquisitive child, yokes the plucking bow string to something hollow and resonant, like a coconut shell. Suddenly the sound is deeper, richer, *thrummier*. Voilà—the first luthier. And for time immemorial, from thousands and thousands of years ago to today, in garages and workshops and factories around

Regal, 1930

the world, the obsessive work of luthiers continues in an attempt to master that seemingly miraculous task of creating beautiful sound from wood and string.

What makes a guitar sound like a guitar? On the one hand, it's kind of simple. Strings are anchored over a resonant wooden "box" with a hole in the center. Stretched tight, the strings vibrate when plucked, and those vibrations start moving the wooden top of the box. And if that wooden top is just the right material planed to just the right thickness, it amplifies the vibrations and adds its own woody flavor until the whole body is acting like a pump pushing out delicious sound waves.

On the other hand, the science is complex, the variables are infinite, and the process is potentially self-destructive. A really well-made acoustic flattop guitar, with the heavy tension of steel strings anchored to a thin wafer of spruce or redwood, is an implosion waiting to happen.

In building a guitar, luthiers start with the body, but for the task of explaining how a guitar works—using the basic all-American steel-string acoustic as the example—it may be best to start with the strings. In legend, Apollo, the famed god of music, invented strings: After slaying a tortoise to make the body of his lyre, Apollo strung it using the poor beast's intestines. (Sheep gut is still used for high-quality strings for violins, violas, and the like.) Guitar strings these days are either steel, with the lower strings wound, or nylon. Thicker strings at the bottom vibrate at a slower frequency, producing a lower sound, or pitch. The thinner treble strings vibrate more quickly, producing a higher sound. Pitch also changes with string length, which is the principle behind tuners and frets. But strings are thin and slip through the air without causing much of a disturbance, and without much of a disturbance, there's not much of a sound wave. For proof, strum an unplugged solid-body electric guitar. Sounds pretty tinny.

That's where the tortoise shell, a.k.a. the body of the guitar, comes in. Through a process called coupling, which describes the joining together of the various parts of the instrument, the guitar body turns the strings' vibration into sound. It's like the old-fashioned song "the thigh bone's connected to the hip bone," with the thigh bone being the bridge, the hip bone being the top, and so on. Glued directly onto the guitar top and consisting of saddle (a white strip of bone or dense synthetic), bridge, bridge pins, and, underneath, the bridge plate, the bridge transmits the strings' vibrations directly to the guitar body. It also has the critical job of affixing the strings to the guitar.

What happens is that the disturbance of the vibrating guitar strings is now transmitted by the bridge to the guitar top, which in turn causes the top to start moving. This thin piece of wood is actually responsible for up to 90 percent of a guitar's tone, presence, sustain, volume, and all the other fun words used to describe

Bronson Honolulu Master, 1958

anatomy of a guitar

The essential parts of an acoustic guitar, as revealed in a typical dreadnought. Note the X-bracing just under the soundhole, how the braces under the top are scalloped, and the configuration of bridge, bridge pins, and saddle. Not visible are the truss rod inside the neck and the particular type of joint that attaches the neck to the guitar body.

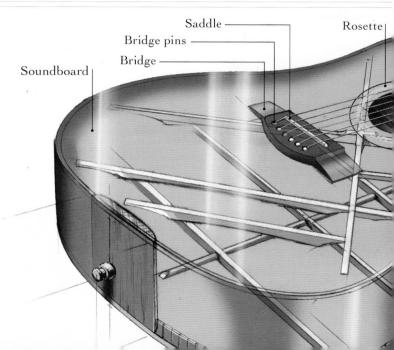

Soundboard

Bridge

Bridge pins

Saddle

Rosette

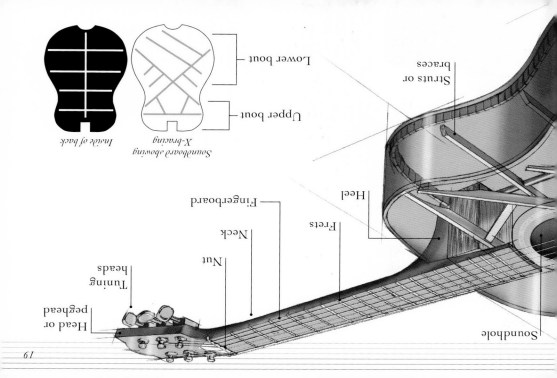

Inside of back

Soundboard showing
X-bracing

Lower bout

Upper bout

Struts or
braces

Heel

Fingerboard

Frets

Neck

Nut

Soundhole

Tuning
heads

Head or
peghead

61

the sound of an individual note or instrument. And we're not talking about the whole top, either. Most of a guitar's "music" is produced by the lower bout, the part of the body below the pinched waist. This is why a cutaway (when one of the guitar's shoulders is cut away so a player has easier access to the upper frets) doesn't adversely affect an acoustic guitar's sound.

Though it may be one of the plainest parts of the guitar, it's in the top that the luthier's skill really shines: in choosing the wood, in planing the boards, in

Martin 00-42, 1935

configuring the bracing underneath. Spruce, with a very high strength-to-weight ratio, is the most commonly used wood for the top. Spruce is also used for violins and piano soundboards. (One intriguing theory that explains why Stradivarius violins sound so distinctive has to do with a mini–Ice Age that occurred from the mid-17th to the early-18th centuries, which caused the alpine spruce trees to grow more slowly, thereby producing denser timber with closely and evenly spaced rings.) Other commonly used soundboard woods are cedar and redwood. For mass-produced, less-expensive guitars, makers often turn to laminates—a fancy name for plywood.

How the top is braced plays an important role as well. Spy under the sound hole with a dentist's mirror, and you'll see an interestingly patterned series of braces or struts. Torres perfected the fan-brace pattern for the classical guitar. Christian Frederick Martin used an "X" brace pattern for the steel-string guitar. Once again, it's about striking a balance: To vibrate effectively, the top needs to be thin, springy, and flat. To stay flat, it needs to be supported by braces. But too much bracing will stifle the vibrations, killing the sound. In quality guitars, the braces will be scalloped—shaved at the edges and the middle for greater lightness and flexibility. In the very best guitars, the luthier will "voice" the top, shaving the braces individually to bring out different qualities of sound, pumping the bass, or sweetening the mids.

What of the rest of the body? In a famous experiment, the father of the modern classical guitar, Antonio de Torres Jurado, constructed a guitar using papier-mâché for the back and sides. The guitar supposedly sounded fantastic. And yet, and yet. . . Guitar geeks talk about woods the way oenophiles obsess over wine. Rosewoods are brilliant, "metallic," rich with overtones, good at reflecting sound. Mahogany is sweet, woody, and balanced. Maple is bright, dry, and dangerously transparent, as it has the unnerving habit of exposing a player's every flaw. Then come the variations: Brazilian rosewood is everything Indian rosewood is, only more so. Koa is like mahogany, but with more midrange. There are also aesthetic considerations, from the bewitchingly

Washburn Style 108, 1892

deep purples and oranges of Brazilian rosewood to the shimmering quality of quilted mahogany. Or is it all tradition for the sake of tradition? Maybe so, when an inventor like Charles Kaman comes along and makes guitar bodies out of an oval scoop of fiberglass. He calls his company Ovation, and lots of performers swear by its guitars.

Another thing Ovation explored was removing the big sound-hole from the center of the guitar and breaking it up into little baby holes scattered around the upper bout. So another myth was shattered: The sound doesn't really come out of that big hole. In fact, it's there to relieve the pressure of air from inside the guitar, particularly from the thumping lower strings. (Vibrations from the treble strings move from bridge to top without stirring much air inside the body.) The fancy name for this phenomenon is Helmholtz resonance; most of us know it as what happens when you blow air across the top of a bottle.

Gibson L-00, 1959

Arguably every detail influences a guitar's voice. Players will swear, for example, that Martin's famous dovetail joint—the joint that attaches the neck to the body—is the reason their guitars boast a legendary warmth, as if it creates a deep wood-to-wood coupling in the heart of the instrument. Players also fuss over the material used in the nut and saddle: Upgrading from synthetics to bone, with their different densities, is said to make a big difference. Players who feel their instrument lacks richness in the bass will swap out plastic bridge pins for wood. But for sustain, try fossilized ivory pins—only $150 a set. Ebony fretboards are said to have a

Gibson Southerner Jumbo, 1951

dampening effect; if you're having a luthier build you a guitar with a small body, go for a rosewood fingerboard. A heavier headstock is said to be better: Modify yours by changing to heavier tuners. On the other hand, a slotted headstock, naturally light because so much of the mass is missing, is said to balance the guitar better; and because the strings come off the tuners at a sharper angle, it adds brightness to the guitar's tone. Some claim it helps carry the sound right up the neck to the player's ears like a chimney drawing smoke. Detail after detail after detail, each subtly affecting those mysterious vibrations.

And then, of course, there are imponderables beyond the reach of even the most gifted luthier. Foremost among these is age. Scour better guitar shops long enough, and you're bound to come upon one of those weird old instruments, say a mahogany-bodied Martin 000-18 from 60 years ago, with cracks, chips, and plugged holes, and with one strum you'll recognize a richness of tone that's as complex as life itself. Was this elusive beauty built into the guitar 60 years ago, or did it just take that long for the varnish to relax and the wood molecules to align themselves properly?

Wood, strings, air—and magic.

BIG BODIES, BIG SOUND

In 1916 Martin built the first dreadnought, fancifully named after a German battleship, in collaboration with the guitar department of the Ditson company, a New York retailer. But the Martin dreadnought didn't really establish itself until the 1930s, when the "D" returned and singers like Gene Autry became entranced by its strong, bassy support for the voice. In 1936 Gibson answered with the Advanced Jumbo, which it marketed as "the original acoustic cannon." Many consider it Gibson's finest flattop.

Martin Ditson, 1916

Gibson Advanced Jumbo, 1938. An estimated 300 were made in the late 1930s. Gibson started making the model again in 1990.

SEASONED WELL

Though chosen first and foremost for its tonal properties, the wood used in acoustic guitars can also be beautiful—or unusual, as in the case of this Fylde, built from discarded single-malt Scotch whiskey casks.

Fylde "Single Malt" Alexander, 2002

AND WELL-SEASONED

The stunning Brazilian rosewood back and sides of Jeff Traugott's 00 model came originally from stumps left over from trees cut 80 years ago.

Jeff Traugott 00, 2003

"The Browson," c. 1910. The fretboard inlay, the delicate rosettes, the snowflake bridge — clearly a labor of love.

1910 EXPERIMENTS

When Joseph Bohmann, originally of Germany, moved
to Chicago and set up his company, he unabashedly
declared himself "The World's Greatest Musical Instrument
Manufacturer." Among Bohmann's unusual creations is this
early "12-string" archtop—six strings on the outside, and
six sympathetic strings running inside the guitar's body.
The unknown builder of "The Browson" tried a different
experiment—he (or she) gave the traditional guitar outline
a twist by designing a massive 17" lower bout.

*Joseph Bohmann acoustic guitar, c.
1910. In addition to the internal strings,
Bohmann offered an early "whammy bar."*

Christian Frederick Martin Sr.

The story of C. F. Martin Sr. is, in many ways, the story of a bridge, of a man whose work, in fact whose lifetime, spanned an old world and a new.

Born in 1796 in Saxony, Germany, in the hillside town of Mark Neukirchen, C. F. Martin was the son of a carpenter who also made guitars on the side. Martin's interest and skills as a luthier must have manifested themselves very early; by the age of 15, he was sent to Vienna,

C. F. Martin Sr., and a 19th-century Martin guitar

200 miles away, to apprentice to one of the world's finest guitar-makers, Johann Stauffer. In addition to being known for the quality of his instruments, Stauffer introduced several innovations: a scroll-shaped headstock with six-on-a-side tuners (this design would look radically modern as Leo Fender echoed it on the Telecaster 150 years later); an extended fingerboard that floated slightly above the guitar top; and a movable neck joint, adjusted by a clock key, that allowed the player to change the neck angle and string height. They were state-of-the-art guitars, for the early 1800s.

In 1825, now a shop foreman with highly refined skills, Martin returned to the family business to make guitars with his father. This incensed the town's Violin Makers' Guild, who wanted to protect their members—in their jealous estimation, the only instrument-related building that the Martins should concern themselves with was making the crates that the violins were shipped in. A turf war ensued, and by 1832 a demoralized C. F. packed up his young family and braved a 100-day voyage in a wooden ship to America.

Martin, 1830s

Cut to the New World and the founding of the first family of American guitars: In 1833 Martin opened C. F. Martin & Company at 196 Hudson Street in New York City. There he sold horns, harps, strings, tuning forks, violin bows, and, of course, guitars, making about one a week in a room in the back. Never quite comfortable in the rough and tumble world of 19th-century New York, the quiet family from Saxony moved to rural Pennsylvania in 1839 and set up shop near the Moravian town of Nazareth, where Martins are made to this day.

By the 1840s, C. F. Martin's genius for guitar design truly blossomed, and he began creating the instruments and innovations that made Martins Martins, and had other American guitar-makers following suit. The pinch-waist German design gave way to a body with a small upper bout and larger lower bout. The fancy Stauffer headstock was replaced by Martin's signature plain rectangular paddle. In fact, plainness ruled, in the bridges and in the decoration around the sound hole.

Martin 6-string, 1870

Most significantly, C. F. Martin developed (and quite possibly invented) the X-bracing pattern under the top that is to this day used in nearly all flattop guitars, save the traditional fan-braced classical guitar. It was Martin's X-brace, which struck exactly the right balance between flexibility and stability, that allowed larger guitars to be created and, ultimately, made it feasible to design a flattop guitar that used steel strings with their greater tension (though Martin didn't offer steel strings as a standard feature until 1922).

C. F. Martin was a complete luthier: a designer, a builder, an innovator, a problem-solver. He also, incidentally, founded one of the longest-running companies in American history. But that kind of longevity would come as no surprise, considering Martin's promise: "We can afford to warrant them, not for a year or a number of years, but for all time."

Martin, 1840s

MARTIN BODY SIZES grew incrementally larger over time—0 to 00 to 000 to D to M to J—with the No. 0 (13½" wide) introduced in 1854 leading up to the first dreadnought (15⅝" wide) in 1916. Expectations of volume grew as well. At the turn of the 19th century, Martin sold its 0 as a concert instrument and the 00 for those in need of "exceptional power." These days a 00 is a quaint parlor size.

Martin 0-21, 1914

Martin Sunburst 00-21, 1951

Martin 000-42, 1918, with ivory bridge and atypical pickguard

Martin OM-18, 1933. OM—orchestra model—was the designation given to a 14-fret 000.

Martin D-28, 1948

THREE TENORS

Tenor guitars have four strings tuned in fifths, giving them a more open sound than a 6-string guitar. They first found success in the late 1920s, when guitars began to replace the tenor banjo as the main rhythm instrument in small jazz bands and dance orchestras. A tenor banjo player could switch to the guitar without having to learn new fingerings. Of course, with the Key Kord you don't have to learn anything—just press down the buttons and it does the fretting for you.

Martin 0-18T, 1930

Lark 3-hole tenor, 1930s

"Just follow the dots
and you can't get into
trouble." — STEVE CROPPER

*Key Kord tenor, c. 1928, with
key box and fretless neck*

SEPARATED AT BIRTH

Once the details snap into focus, it's clear that these are not twins. But even a Martin lover might be surprised to learn that more than 30 years separate the pearly 0-42 and classical music teacher Vahdah Olcott Bickford's personal 2-44. They really *do* build them the way they used to.

Martin 0-42, c. 1898

Martin 2-44, the Olcott Bickford Artist Model, 1930

Gibson Everly Brothers,
1968

"IN OUR IMAGE"

The Everly Brothers' close harmony work made them a pop sensation in the early 1960s, and by 1962 they endorsed a Gibson guitar similar to the original J-200. Believe it or not, the symmetrical pickguards on this late model (1968) are actually restrained compared to the sound-deadening amount of pickguard used in the original version. The brothers' father, the country star Ike Everly, designed the oversized bridge.

INNOVATORS

Some of the finest instruments of the prewar era were neither Martins nor Gibsons, but guitars built in Chicago by two Swedish immigrants, Carl and August Larson. Sold under a variety of names—Larson, Maurer, Stahl, Euphonon, and Prairie State—Larsons are beautifully crafted instruments, many of which feature the brothers' patented laminated X-bracing and a curious internal steel-rod bracing system. Experts believe the Larsons made about 2,000 instruments in all.

Larson Stahl,
1920

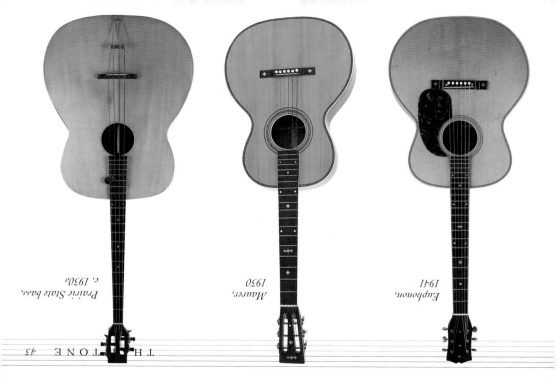

Prairie State bass, c. 1930s

Maurer, 1930

Euphonon, 1941

SHAPE-SHIFTERS

Gretsch, who manufactured
a variety of musical
instruments, had an inside
track on the culture's
transition from banjo to
guitar in the late 1920s, and
created the Rhumba to appeal
to banjo players. Washburn,
with its not-quite-a-Martin
reputation, went upscale to
create the Bell, with a shape
intended to provide a new
kind of sound and tickle
the ears of discriminating
players. Both were very
short-lived.

*Gretsch Rhumba,
c. 1933*

Washburn "Bell" style 5271,
c. 1929

FUNKY ARCHTOPS

You might see them by the ones and twos hanging in the back of the guitar store, 50-year-old archtops that were never rare or valuable to begin with and are today thin-sounding curiosities to players whose ears are attuned to the sustain, overtones, and richness of a well-made flattop. Even the story they tell has as much to do with marketing as music, like banjo companies Bacon & Day and S. S. Stewart trying to catch the jazz guitar wave unleashed by Gibson.

Armstrong Dansant, c. 1959

Bacon & Day Troubador, 1930s

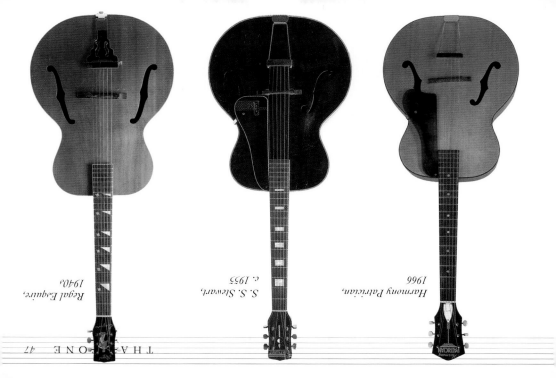

Regal Esquire,
1940s

S. S. Stewart,
c. 1955

Harmony Patrician,
1966

HOW AN ARCHTOP WORKS

Acoustic archtop guitars look different, sound different, and work differently than flattop guitars. Created by Orville Gibson and brought to its first artistic peak, the Gibson L-5, by luthier Lloyd Loar, archtop design comes out of the violin family. In the traditional archtops of the jazz age, the top and back are carved out of thick boards, f-holes are used in place of a round center hole, and two parallel tone bars brace the top. Also, instead of being pinned directly into the bridge, the strings drape over the

Regal Esquire, 1940s

bridge and are held in place by a tailpiece. When played, the soundboard moves up and down and the pressure is implosive, forcing the body in on itself. Archtops have a mellow, smooth character but are capable of great punch and cutting power— necessary when pounding out the rhythm in a big-band context. And traditionally, archtops project sound, unlike a flattop, which envelops the player in sound.

Contemporary luthiers are returning to archtop design, but lightening the tops and using X-bracing to create ravishing, versatile instruments that respond to fingerpicking as well as comping, and offer some of the warmth and sustain of flattop guitars.

WHAT WERE THEY THINKING?

This rare Vega Cremona is actually an archtop (the wood pressed on a form, not hand-carved). And look closely: Those are f-holes with pickguards added on. Costing nearly as much as the acoustically far superior Gibson L-5, this offering from the Vega banjo company was your basic lemon.

Vega Cremona, 1952

Roy Rogers with Trigger guitar, 1950s

NOVELTY GUITARS rode the wave of two long-standing musical fads, the Hawaiian guitar of island stars like Sol Hoopii, and the "singing cowboy" trend created by Gene Autry and others. The older instruments, though cheap and sold through places like the Sears catalog, were real wood. Later on they devolved into little more than children's toys, made out of pressed cardboard or plastic.

The Lone Ranger, c. 1930s, capitalizing on the popular characters that appeared first on radio, then television

Slide Princess, set up for Hawaiian playing, 1930s

"Hawaiian" guitar with full sunset, 1930s

Stella 12-string, 1930s, sold under the Sovereign label

Ciani 12-string, early 20th century. Ciani was John D'Angelico's uncle and first teacher.

Guild F-212, 1979

Landola-made Espana 6-12
Double-Neck, 1970

THE CLANGING OF THE BELLS is how Pete Seeger
described the bright, chimey sound of a 12-
string guitar. Though its origins are obscure and
its temperament is notoriously fickle (not only
difficult to tune, but terribly prone to warpage),
the 12-string's distinctive chorus sound has
contributed to every form of popular music, from
the blues of Leadbelly to the folk-rock of The
Byrds. "Stairway to Heaven" anyone?

JOHN'S VS. GEORGE'S

On September 10, 1962,
John Lennon and George
Harrison took possession of
brand-new sunburst Gibson
J-160Es. The next day,
Lennon used his to record
"Love Me Do." Though
inferior acoustically because
of its ladder bracing, the
model made stunning history
by being used throughout
The Beatles' career. Lennon's
was his second—the first was
stolen during a Christmas
show in 1963. He added the
caricatures during a 1968
Bed-In with Yoko.

*John Lennon's Gibson J-160E,
1964, after several refinishes*

George Harrison's Gibson
J-160E, 1962

THIS MACHINE KILLS FASCISTS

Woody Guthrie, legendary American folksinger and songwriter, owned hundreds of guitars in his life, many of which he freely gave away to other musicians. Here's a typical Guthrie guitar: a beat-up Martin 00-18 (he favored small-bodied mahogany instruments because they were inexpensive) that Woody blithely customized with his name and favorite slogan.

Martin 00-18, 1937, owned by Woody Guthrie

Guthrie scratched his name on the back, along with "this machine kills fascists."

TOOLS OF THE ARTIST

Bob Dylan's probably performed with
thousands of guitars in his career.
Here's one of his many Martins.
Hank Williams is best known for
using a Gibson Southern Jumbo and
a Martin D-28 (whose current owner
is Neil Young), but this J-50 was also
one of his. Willie Nelson, on the other
hand, has been remarkably faithful to
just one instrument, his world-famous
Trigger. He's played a hole right into
the top—which also has signatures
of more than 100 artists and friends,
including Leon Russell, Roger Miller,
Kris Kristofferson, Gene Autry,
Johnny Cash, and Waylon Jennings.

*Martin 00-17, 1949—
Bob Dylan's plain
mahogany-bodied
Martin*

*Gibson J-50,
c. 1947, belonging
to Hank Williams*

*Martin N-20,
"Trigger," 1969*

"I've never found
anything as good to me,
for what I was trying to
get, as Trigger. I could
play it acoustically,
I can run it through an
amp. It still gets a great
sound."

—WILLIE NELSON

GREATS *Bob Dylan*

B ob Dylan would appear on few lists of great guitarists. As he himself said, "I'm not an artist. Segovia is an artist. I'm a poet." But he understood the power of the guitar as well as anyone. Early on, he embodied the modern troubadour with his scuffed-up J-45, strings akimbo, perfectly suited to the vigorously rough-edged style of playing on those first records. You can hear what he learned at a young age from those street corner bluesmen, and the very image of a young Bob would inspire a generation of singer-songwriters.

Then, on the night of July 25, 1965, Dylan harnessed every subversive ounce of the electric guitar by plugging in a Stratocaster at the Newport Folk Festival. A few years later the chameleon would change again, and a guitar would be the signifier: There's "country" Bob, toting a spiffy Gibson SJ-200, ornately tooled as a cowboy boot, on the cover of *Nashville Skyline*. There may be no other player so adept at wielding the guitar's genius as a vehicle for self-expression. "I could sing *Porgy and Bess* with two chords, G and D, and still get the story across." This is not to say that Dylan's got no chops. Listen to "Buckets of Rain." His playing is surpassingly beautiful.

Hofner 491, 1966

Harmony Sovereign, 1971, borrowing a few ideas from Rickenbacker

Guild F-50, 1960s

Harmony 167 Folk, 1968

Eko P2 Angela, 1963

HOOTENANNY TIME

Launched in 1958 with The Kingston Trio's unexpected hit "Tom Dooley," America's folk revival turned into a folk boom. And everybody wanted to sing along. "Guitars hit a cashbox crescendo," *Business Week* reported, and guitar-makers of every stripe rushed to put an instrument in people's hands, from high-end Guilds, folk machines for the serious strummer, to the odd budget Eko with its floating bridge, trapeze tailpiece, and slotted headstock.

Recording King,
1939

Regal Recording King,
1930s

RECORDING WHO?

In the later Depression years, Gibson, Kay, and other companies made guitars to be sold through the Montgomery Ward department store chain under the boastful name of "Recording King." Some, like the Ray Whitley, named after the popular cowboy singer and B-Western movie star, were quite fancy, featuring rosewood back and sides.

Ray Whitley Recording King, probably made by Gibson, 1939

A SMART MOVE

Epiphone rode the jazz age
wave of banjo playing, then
in the late '20s introduced
the Recording line of guitars;
perfect timing, given that
the 1929 stock market crash
effectively ended the Roaring
'20s and the reign of the tenor
banjo. Oddly, the unusual
cutaway Recording D was
the typical Epiphone guitar.
The full-bodied Recording E
is extremely rare.

*Epiphone Recording D, 1928 —
clearly a well-played instrument.*

Epiphone Recording E, 1929
Note the staggered bridge pins.

PRETTY . . . is not the typical message of a serious musical instrument, where form inevitably follows function. But the guitar always had a flashy side, even before the hot rod electrics of the 1960s. Check out the knight-like motif on the Old Kraftsman fretboard and the graphically stunning use of dominoes on the black Le Domino from the early 1930s.

Gibson Kel Kroydon, 1931

Kay Kraft Style B, 1939

Old Craftsman "Crown,"
1941

Le Domino 4010,
1932

Gibson Nick Lucas,
1928

Euphonon, c. 1940

... AND PRETTIER

Though "fancier" is a better word for this pair of beauties, from the very showy wide-bodied Euphonon with the heavy purfling and symmetrical engraved see-through pickguards, to the top-of-the-line Nick Lucas with its "Florentine" engraved fretboard and headstock.

OTHER MATERIALS

The first pure ingot of aluminum was
extracted in 1855 and exhibited at the
Paris Exposition. By 1886, an American
named Neil Merrill was experimenting
with musical instruments using
the metal. His catalog boasted this
innovation as "the greatest
musical invention of the
age . . . possess[ing] a
volume, purity and
richness of tone
impossible in the all-
wood instruments."
Or perhaps not,
considering that his
guitar is a museum
curiosity.

*Merrill Style A, 1895, with an aluminum
back visible through the sound hole*

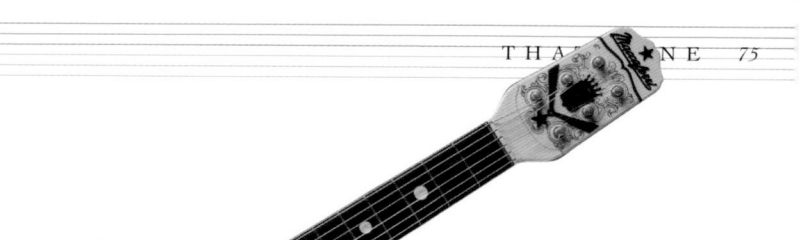

Maccaferri plastic guitar, 1950s

MARIO MACCAFERRI unveiled the plastic guitar in 1953 after his hugely best-selling all-plastic ukulele was adopted by Arthur Godfrey. Featuring a number of design innovations (warp-proof through-neck that could be adjusted with a simple screwdriver), it's a guitar that wanted to be taken seriously, but it never rose above being treated as a serious toy.

GREATS *Joni Mitchell*

A masterful singer, a peerless songwriter, composer, painter, and restless innovator. All describe Joni Mitchell. But she is also a highly original guitarist who truly thinks outside the box in her approach to the instrument. As a child, she taught herself the guitar through a Pete Seeger tutorial, but later developed her own idiosyncratic system: Instead of bringing her musical gifts to the guitar, with its standard tunings and typical C's and D's and F# minors, she would fiddle for hours with the tuning pegs until she found a sound that matched her mood. This resulted in her using some 50 different nonstandard tunings in writing her songs, creating a vocabulary of sound that she calls her "weird chords." Interestingly, with echoes of Django Reinhardt here and his own damaged fretting hand, it is said that Joni Mitchell started using unique tunings to compensate for a weakness in her left hand caused by childhood polio; fretting the usual chord shapes was just too strenuous. There is also an artist's rebellion: "Why is it," she once said, "that Americans need to hear their happiness major and their tragedy minor, and as jazzy as they can handle is a seventh chord? Are they not experiencing complex emotions?"

Gibson Hummingbird,
1961

BIRDS OF A FEATHER

Gibson met the folk boom head-on with a variety of models, including two square-shouldered dreadnoughts designed to compete with Martins. Introduced in 1960, the beloved Hummingbird quickly evolved into a short-scale, mahogany-bodied dreadnought. Two years later, the fancier Dove arrived, featuring a maple body, longer scale (25½"), and brighter sound. Note the bridge with its mother-of-pearl dove shapes.

Gibson Dove,
1963

BLUES KINGS

Starting in the late 1920s, Gibson introduced three affordable small-bodied guitars, the L-0, L-00 (not widely available until 1932), and L-1, famously used by Robert Johnson. Lightly built, they had a warm, responsive tone and surprising volume, perfect for fingerpicking blues and ragtime. The Sunburst L-00 probably sold for $25 when it was new.

Gibson L-1, c. 1928

Gibson Sunburst L-00, c. 1933.
Reissued in the 1990s, it is officially
called The Blues King.

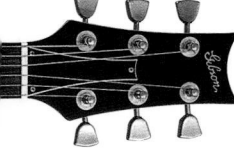

*Gibson Mark 53,
1978*

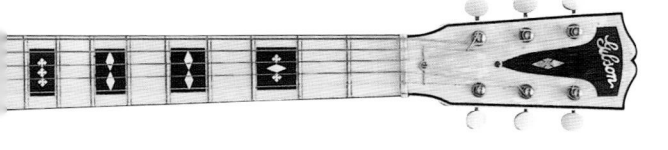

*Gibson LC-Century,
1933*

A RESTLESS INNOVATOR, Gibson found inspiration everywhere. But not necessarily success. The LC-Century commemorated the Century of Progress in 1933; the extensive use of "mother-of-toilet-seat" pearloid made it much better to look at than to play. In the 1970s, Gibson introduced the scientifically designed Mark line of flattops whose specs derived from acoustical research (rather than old-fashioned, luthier-inspired trial and error). Despite the '70s groovy look and supposedly superior bracing patterns, Gibson discontinued the series after four years.

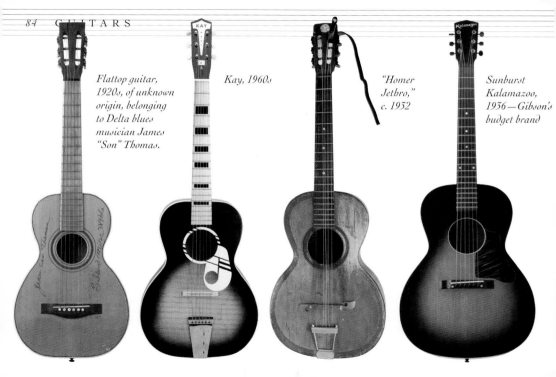

Flattop guitar, 1920s, of unknown origin, belonging to Delta blues musician James "Son" Thomas.

Kay, 1960s

"Homer Jethro," c. 1952

Sunburst Kalamazoo, 1936 — Gibson's budget brand

THE PEOPLE'S INSTRUMENT

Even going back centuries, the guitar had a split personality—a home in both the king's private salon and the corner tavern. In America, almost anyone who wanted a guitar could afford one—a page from the 1908 Sears catalog lists guitars starting at $1.89. Then again, if you couldn't, there was nothing stopping you from making your own—like the "Homer Jethro," belonging to the Country Hall of Famers Homer & Jethro, a.k.a. "the thinking man's hillbillies."

Stella Sundale, 1955

Serenade guitar, 1930s, belonging to Billy Cox, the "Dixie Songbird"

GREATS *Robert Johnson*

With his gutsy songs, keening voice, and masterful guitar work, this quintessential Delta blues musician would influence everyone from Elvis Presley to Eric Clapton to The Rolling Stones and Led Zeppelin. But what also sets Robert Johnson apart is the mystery: He is the man who in legend went to the crossroads and sold his soul to the devil in order to play the guitar. While performing, he often turned his back, as if he didn't want the audience to see what he was doing. A cataract gave him the look of one with the evil eye, and he had the unnerving gift of being able to hear a piece of music just once and later be able to play and sing it perfectly. Then there's his death: poisoned, at the age of 27, by a jealous husband. But for all the hoodoo, Johnson in fact was a well-traveled, well-liked, well-connected musician who mastered the blues guitar idiom—tight riffs and propulsive rhythms, slides, bends, turn-arounds, open tunings, and repeated motifs—and wrote a small but potent body of work; his complete recordings include 29 songs.

RADICAL DEPARTURE

Charles Kaman, an
aeronautical engineer
and jazz guitarist,
revolutionized the acoustic
guitar when he launched
Ovation in 1966. This
early instrument looks
like any dreadnought
from the front—but
turn it over, and find the
signature synthetic back
molded in the shape of a
parabolic bowl, designed
to improve the guitar's
balance and projection,
and make it stronger and
more rugged overall.

*Ovation Balladeer,
1967*

Bowl back of Balladeer, made of composite plastic

SIGNATURES

There's just something about country musicians and signed guitars. Hank Snow did it up right on his custom Gibson with the cherry burst, hummingbird pickguard, and detailing around every conceivable outline. In 1933, singing cowboy superstar Gene Autry ordered the first-ever D-45 from Martin. Autry was just coming off a huge hit with "That Silver-Haired Daddy of Mine"—what a way to celebrate. A guy named Elvis—you may have heard of him?—preferred to DIY it, using stick-on metal letters to customize his Martin D-18 (following page). Somewhere along the way the "s" went missing.

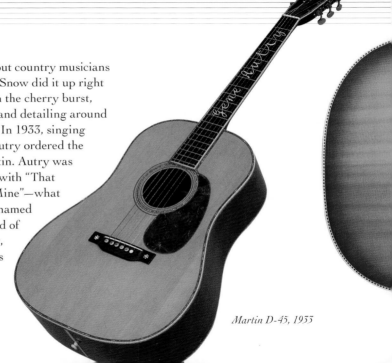

Martin D-45, 1933

Custom Gibson, 1961, belonging to Hank Snow, the Country Music Hall of Famer who made some 840 commercial recordings

WALLY GEORGE: "When will you write more songs?"
ELVIS: "That's all a hoax. I can't even read music."
GEORGE: "What about your guitar?"
ELVIS: "Can't play it—use it as a brace."

*Elvis Presley's D-18, 1942,
clearly showing signs of his
banging rhythm style*

CROSSING OVER

Two companies almost
exclusively known for their
electric guitars started
dabbling in acoustics during
the folk boom. The Fender
carries over several design
elements from its electric
cousins, notably the Strat-
inspired headstock and
intonation-adjustable metal
bridge with individual saddles.
The 1960 Rickenbacker is
quite the looker with its ornate
bridge, pearly pickguards,
winged headstock, and
herringbone trim.

Fender Palomino, 1970

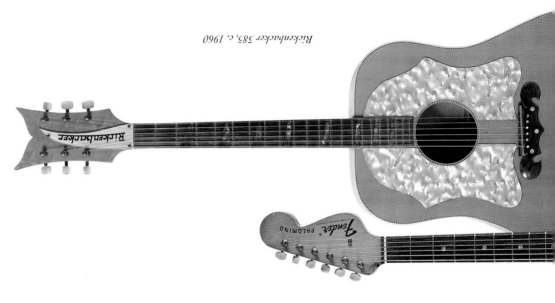

Rickenbacker 385, c. 1960

NEW KID ON THE BLOCK

Bob Taylor started fooling with guitars—not playing, but constructing and deconstructing—as a kid. By the time he was in high school, he made his first acoustic guitars using a book for a teacher. Today, Taylor Guitar, cofounded with Kurt Listug in 1974, is one of the largest, most prestigious guitar-makers in the world.

Bob Taylor 12th-grade guitar (front and back), c. 1972, one of the guitars Taylor made while still in high school. The abalone inlay comes from shells that he harvested himself from the nearby Pacific.

Taylor GSRS, 2000 — a bigger and bolder Taylor, the "Grand Symphony"

Taylor 814CE, 2000, a rosewood Taylor with Venetian cutaway. Taylors are known for their thin, easy-to-play necks—and neck joints that don't require the unsaive surgery of a dovetail to reset.

TWO

Louder!

Prairie State "F," 1930

FINDING ITS VOICE

or centuries, guitarists managed just fine with their soft-spoken instruments. After all, they either played alone, wandering the hills like Hector Berlioz, the composer who also loved the guitar; accompanied singers or dancers in the local tavern; or noodled around the campfire while cattle lowed in the background. (Beginning in the 1700s, Spaniards brought their guitars with them to the vast American Southwest.) Even when rigged up with steel strings, like early Martins, the traditional acoustic guitar was comparatively quiet. Today we call these small-bodied instruments parlor guitars and praise them for their intimacy. Before World War I, that was pretty much it.

This quality, however, also isolated the guitarist. Before the 1920s, the typical guitar just didn't play well with others. The piano drowned it out.

Gibson L-1 Artist, 1906

So did reeds, woodwinds, and brasses, inhibiting the guitar's use as a voice in classical music. The same was true for the day's pop. By the 19-teens, Gibson, inventors of the gorgeous "F" and "A" mandolins, helped fuel a national trend of mandolin mania by sponsoring mandolin orchestras. Old photographs of these happy groups often reveal one or two glum-looking guitarists, their instruments about to be overpowered by the bright, chirpy sound of a dozen or more mandolins. And when mandolin mania finally petered out in the early '20s, America elected as its new favorite stringed instrument the tenor banjo, whose bone-piercing twang showed no mercy to the guitar. (Even today, the very word *banjo* makes many a guitarist cringe, and a particularly powerful bluegrass dreadnought is often given the epithet "banjo-killer.")

Neither the advent of commercial radio (1919) nor that of recorded phonographs (1925) helped, despite starting a revolution in how people listened to music. Primitive recording required music to be played really loudly and up close to the microphone. Put a group of musicians together and the guitar disappeared.

In the language of evolution, it was time for the guitar to adapt. Thus began a quest that defined the guitar for decades to come: the quest for volume. Volume doesn't just mean loudness, the filling-rattling sound of Nigel Tufnel's amp cranked up to "11." It's much more vital, like oxygen to a fire. Without finding more volume, the guitar could easily have descended into a permanent state of being a minor, solo instrument. But in finding volume, the guitar slowly roared into preeminence.

Volume created new guitars that then created new music. The dreadnought begat the country singer, which begat the singer-songwriter phenomenon. The big archtop begat the jazz guitar, which begat Charlie Christian, one of the fathers of bebop. Hawaiian guitar begat the first electric guitar, which begat the Les Pauls, Telecasters, and Strats (and their significant offshoot, the Fender electric bass), which begat rock, pop, R&B, funk, reggae, metal, punk, and the Nashville sound.

How the quest unfolded is a bit like a family tree, with limbs emanating from the single trunk called volume. Acoustic flattop builders such as Martin took the path of steel strings, bigger and

Oahu Deluxe Jumbo 68, c. 1936

deeper bodies, refined building techniques (particularly in the forward-shifting and strategic shaving of braces), and the occasional experiment with amplifying devices like the Selmer Maccaferri with its internal resonator. The idiosyncratic and innovative Gibson drew on the principles of violin construction to invent the archtop guitar, perfecting it with the 1924 L-5, which possessed an ability to cut through the group and be heard (bye-bye, tenor banjo!).

Working on a very different limb was the prolifically inventive Czech immigrant John Dopyera, who created the "ampliphonic" guitar. More commonly known as a resonator, this style of guitar uses one or more spun aluminum cones that are built into the guitar's body and work much like the cone inside a speaker, mechanically amplifying the sound. Dopyera's first, the National, had a metal body to make it even louder. After business complications, Dopyera and his brothers next founded a company called Dobro and

Gibson L-4, with oval hole, 1920s

developed the wooden-bodied, single-cone instrument, now generically known as the dobro and essential to bluegrass and other old-timey music.

And then, of course, came the biggest change of all, as guitar-makers began to harness the relatively new idea of electrical amplification that was then being developed by the radio industry. Crude pickups began appearing on musical instruments throughout the 1920s, with the first commercially advertised electric guitar, made by the Stromberg-Voisinet company, arriving in 1928. Signal strength was still a major problem, though, and any sort of electric guitar didn't catch on until 1932, when Adolph Rickenbacker—curiously, a die and tool man who supplied spun cones and other parts for the Dopyeras—introduced the "Frying Pan," an electric Hawaiian-style guitar (played flat on the lap).

Four years later Gibson released the ES-150, now known as the Charlie Christian guitar, and made history.

Epiphone Century, 1952

Slingerland Cathedranola Sammy Mussmanno, c. 1954, which uses a spruce disk for a resonator

Fender Telecaster, 1950s

The guitar was never not heard again.

guitar: Leo Fender, of Fender, and his epoch-changing Broadcaster. to introduce the first commercially successful solid-body electric to them in 1946, paving the way for another man and another company passed on putting the guitar into production when Les Paul brought it

In one of those "What were they thinking?" moments, Gibson guitar shape. added the two halves of a split Epiphone, just to give the beast a familiar 4″ × 4″ pine plank on which he mounted two pickups and around which were creating the first solid-body electric. Known as "The Log," it consisted of a inventor Les Paul solved the problem of unwanted hollow-body feedback by evolutionary hurdle was accomplished in the mid-1940s, when guitarist and this instrument brought "Spanish" guitar into the modern age. The final

With the ES standing for "Electro-Spanish" and the 150 for how much it cost (significantly less than its fancy cousin, the Gibson Super 400),

BIGGER IS LOUDER ... IN FLATTOPS ...

Tops in the size category clearly belongs to this Larson Brothers' Prairie State behemoth with a whopping 21" wide body. (A classic Martin dreadnought, by comparison, is 15⅝".) The Larsons also created a 19" custom-cutaway for country star Jay Rich. Oahu offered this tastefully ornate Hawaiian guitar—with a raised nut and square neck—and called it a Deluxe Jumbo 68.

Larson Brothers Prairie State custom, c. 1935

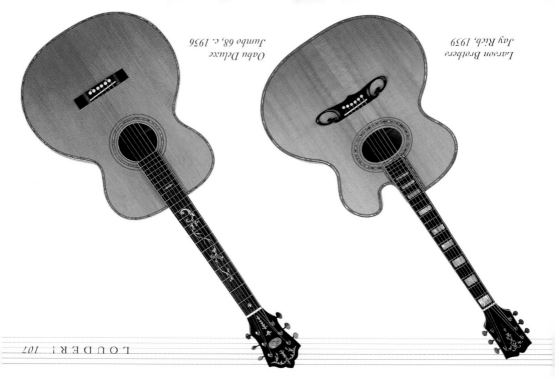

Larson Brothers
Jay Rich, 1939

Oahu Deluxe
Jumbo 68, c. 1936

... IN ARCHTOPS, with large models from Prairie State (its only f-hole guitar) and Kay, another Chicago manufacturer, who introduced this hefty archtop with a two-tone fingerboard in the early '40s. Gibson proved forever that bigger is better with its flagship Super 400, an 18" wide jazz monster that supplanted the L-5.

Prairie State "F,"
1930

Kay K-40,
1941

"It is worth any sacrifice made for its possession."—GIBSON, TOUTING THE SUPER 400

Gibson Super 400, 1935

...EVEN RESONATORS

With the cone functioning as an amplifier, National didn't need to make bigger guitars to make louder guitars. In fact, their smaller and thus easier to handle size was touted as an asset for the working musician. But someone at National caught the size bug when designing this wide-body.

National Aragon De Luxe, c. 1938

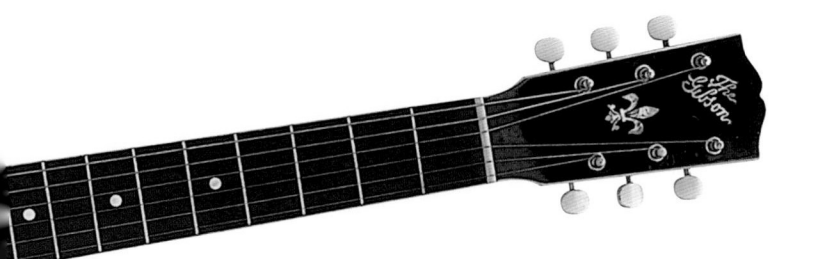

Gibson "O," 1920. Note the extended fingerboard on the treble side.

THE GIBSON "O"

The direct descendent of Orville Gibson's original carved-top guitar, the Style O lasted until the advent of the epoch-making L-5. The extraordinary single-cutaway with the Florentine scroll appeared in 1908–1909.

Orville Gibson

Just as every modern steel-string flattop guitar owes its existence to the work of C. F. Martin more than a century ago, so too is every archtop, acoustic or electric, indebted to the brief but brilliant career of Orville Gibson, an eccentric musical inventor who just saw things differently from everyone else.

Gibson's singular breakthrough was to apply violin-making techniques to guitars and mandolins. But how he arrived at this breakthrough is a bit of a mystery. Unlike Martin, who came from a line of instrument-makers, Gibson just

appeared, a shoe clerk and restaurant worker in Kalamazoo, Michigan, who spent his spare time pursuing interests in music and woodworking. Eventually he acquired a cramped 10' × 12' shop from which began to emerge the most glorious procession of musical instruments: curlicued, scrolled, and sculpted, glittering with abalone and mother-of-pearl, uniquely conceived and elegant in their execution.

He invented not only the archtop guitar and classic American mandolins but also a menagerie of hybrids, including the harp guitar, harp zither, and lyre mandolin, whose neoclassical image was used in early Gibson labels. As a final exotic touch, many instruments featured a gleaming star and crescent moon inlay on the headstock, the work of a Turkish pearl cutter who lived nearby.

Gibson applied for and received only one patent in his career, for a mandolin (he was still working in a local restaurant at the time). It sums up his philosophy of instrument-making—wood to be "carved . . . to leave the layer-grains in the same position they occupied in natural growth."

Hand-carved Orville Gibson guitar, 1897 (front and back)

He continued exuberantly: "Every portion of the woody structure seems to be alive with emphatic sound at every touch of the instrument—a character and quality of sound entirely new to this class of musical instruments, and which cannot be imparted to others by a description in words."

By the turn of the 20th century these seductive Gibsons found not only acceptance, after initial ridicule, but a fair measure of success, attracting five local lawyers and businessmen who thought it would be a good idea to turn Gibson into a proper company. On October 11, 1902, they officially launched the Gibson Mandolin-Guitar Manufacturing Company, Limited. Orville Gibson was not among the five; instead, always the eccentric, he arranged to sell his patent, and died never knowing how profound his impact was in the world of guitars and music.

Orville Gibson guitar, 1898, clearly showing the colored layer-grains of wood. Note also the oval sound hole and basic headstock shape that is still used by Gibson today—datable, however, by the exotic crescent moon and star inlay.

WHAT THE "L"?

Round holes, oval holes, f-holes, name changes, and endless stylistic tweaks across the instrument: Over the years Gibson produced a bewildering number of acoustic "L" archtops, as the company sought to put the fruits of its expertise into every player's hands, at every price point.

Custom-painted Gibson L-4, c. 1920

Gibson L-1, early 20th century

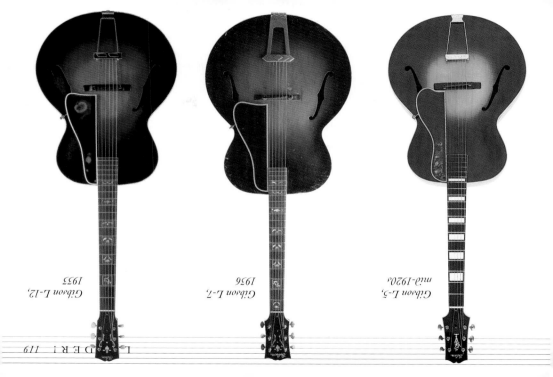

Gibson L-12,
1933

Gibson L-7,
1936

Gibson L-5,
mid-1920s

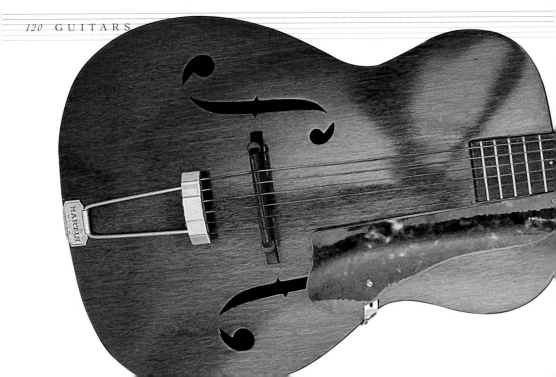

Martin R-17, c. 1954

FOLLOWING SUIT

Martin reluctantly followed Gibson into the archtop world in 1931. And a good thing, too, as its C and R models helped the company survive the Depression. But, while Martin flattops of the period are considered the finest ever made, its archtops—like this all-mahogany R-17, with its pressed rather than carved top and back—are more of a curiosity.

GREATS *Maybelle Carter*

To learn of "Mother Maybelle's" adventures with The Carter Family is to realize how quickly life changed in the 20th century. In 1927, Maybelle (far left), Sara, and A. P. Carter, along with hundreds of other hopefuls (including Jimmie Rodgers), descended from the hollows of Appalachia to Bristol, Tennessee, where a man named Ralph Peer installed an exotic recording machine in a local hotel. Those "Bristol Sessions" marked the birth of country music. Forty years later, Maybelle was performing with her daughters on her son-in-law's national TV program, *The Johnny Cash Show*. A self-taught musician, she revolutionized country and folk guitar with her innovative style, "the Carter Scratch." Through this rich, bouncy technique—plucking out the melody with her thumb on the bass and middle strings, and strumming the chords on the treble strings—Maybelle Carter essentially introduced the guitar as *the* lead instrument in country music. Pretty much every folk guitarist borrowed from her as well. How did it come about? "When I started playing the guitar," she said, "I didn't have nobody to play with me, so that's how I developed the style of kicking in the rhythm too."

BRACES PLUS

This exquisite parlor guitar from the late 1800s was devised by William B. Tilton, a violin-maker who invented a device called "Tilton's Improvement"—an innovative resonating system comprised of the unusual tailpiece, the disk visible through the sound hole, and a long wooden tonebar inside the body. The Larson Brothers worked to improve the tone and volume of this flattop with interior longitudinal bars designed to take the stress off the top, freeing it to sing loud and clear.

William B. Tilton guitar, late 1800s

Larson Brothers 12-fret slothead guitar, mid-1930s

HIS MASTER'S LICKS

The original resonator guitar, from 1920, evolved out of John Matthias Augustus Stroh's acoustic work of the 19th century. Tackling the problem of how to amplify a violin, Stroh replaced the instrument's "body" with a vibrating diaphragm attached to a megaphone. The result is just like an early phonograph. He patented the idea in 1899, and there are Stroh violins, violas, cellos, mandolins, and guitars.

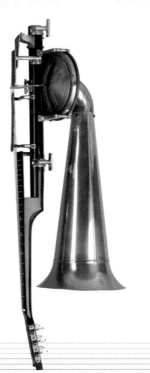

George Evans and Co. Stroh Hawaiian, 1920s. The George Evans company took over the manufacturing of Stroh instruments at the turn of the century and made these unusual instruments until 1942.

GREATS *Django Reinhardt*

The gypsy jazz genius is one of the most startlingly original musicians ever to play the guitar. Growing up on the outskirts of Paris, he picked up an early musical education in violin and six-string banjo in the city's cafés. Then, when he was 18, Django accidentally set fire to his caravan. He and his wife escaped with their lives, but the fire nearly cost him a leg and fused the third and fourth fingers of his left hand. It took Django a year to recover, during which time two central events occurred. One, he taught himself to play the guitar with a unique fingering system, and two, according to legend, he discovered American jazz through a recording of Louis Armstrong's "Dallas Blues." By the 1930s Django was leading Le Quintette du Hot Club de France, playing some of the swingingest jazz ever heard, astonishing listeners with his trills and octaves, double-stops and arpeggios, blazing fast runs and muscular comping. He also composed a number of timeless jazz standards, including "Nuages" and "Djangology." Yet some days he'd rather go fishing. Literally. With the bearing of a natural aristocrat, Django never practiced or learned to read music, and showed up for gigs only when he felt like it.

DJANGO'S AX

Mario Maccaferri was a classical guitarist, a luthier, and a pioneer in the use of plastics. He invented the plastic guitar in the 1950s (see page 75). Decades before, he teamed up with the French saxophone-maker Selmer to produce a line of innovative instruments, including the distinctive d-hole steel-string Orchestre model that Django Reinhardt made world famous. Curiously, one of Maccaferri's key designs was a patented internal resonator of such doubtful effect that guitarists either had it removed or ordered their instruments without the option.

*Selmer Maccaferri
Orchestre, 1932*

THE NAME DOPYERA travels like a vine through 20th-century guitar history. John Dopyera invented the resonator guitar and cofounded the National String Instrument Company. After deep differences, John and his brothers founded the Dobro company—the name derived from Dopyera Brothers and means "good" in their native Czechoslovakian. Made with both metal and wood bodies, Dobros are essential to bluegrass and are used in blues, jazz, slide, and more.

Dobro M/16/S, 1934

Custom headstock

A humbler Dobro, date unknown

THE DOBRO VINE CONTINUES through the big Chicago-based company Regal, which licensed the Dobro and at one point split the country along the Mississippi. Regal got the east.

Regal #27, mid-1930s

Dobro Model 12 "Ye Olde Wooden" 12-string, 1974

BUT IS IT LEGAL?

Considering the sound put out by a typical 6-string Dobro, players joke that you might need a license to carry a 12-string. This one was from John Dopyera's personal collection.

BEAUTY AND THE BEAST

This shimmering National Tri-Cone was owned by the celebrated bluesman and bottleneck specialist Tampa Red (his name's engraved on the lower bout). On the right, a Duolian turned into a piece of folk art by someone whose initials are "A. R." Custom-painted to within an inch of its life, from the marbleized headstock to the keyhole western scene on the back, it even has a repainted logo.

*National Style 4
"Chrysanthemum" Tri-Cone,
1928*

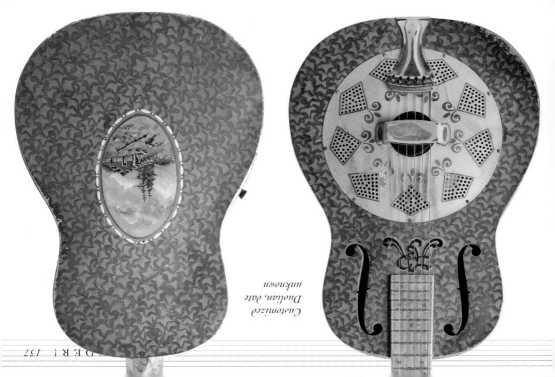

*Customized
Duolian, date
unknown*

Martin Paramount Style L, 1930s

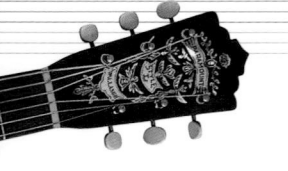

DOUBLED-UP

In the early 1930s, Martin made 36 unusual instruments for William L. Lange's Paramount brand. In this Style L model, it's as if the regular body is nested in a larger body, which acts like a banjo-style resonator. Leo Master did the same thing with much more decorative effect.

Leo Master, 1930s

HAWAIIAN GUITAR

It's hard to overestimate the importance of Hawaiian (or "steel") guitar. Even harder, perhaps, to convince listeners saturated by late-20th-century pop to believe that that corny, swooping sound could have had such a profound influence on American guitar. But it did: Hawaiian guitar gave us the solo guitarist—and the guitar "solo"—and pretty much single-handedly forced the invention of the electric guitar so that the soloist could be better heard. The Rickenbacker "Frying Pan" was designed to sit in the lap of a superstar like Sol Hoopii.

Though guitars first came to Hawaii in the hands of missionaries, Mexican cowboys who worked the ranches, and travelers from California, the significant event happened around 1865, when shipwrecked Portuguese sailors appeared with their steel-string guitars. Hawaiians fell in love with the sound and the instrument. And without any kind of formal training, they were free to experiment with tunings, creating "slack key" guitar—where the tuning keys are "slackened" until strumming open strings produces a chord, most often a G.

Cut to Joseph Kekeku, widely credited with inventing slide guitar, who as a guitar-crazy 11-year-old picked up a rusty bolt—the first "steel"?—while walking along some train tracks and slid it across the strings. What a sound! It was sweet, it was supple, it echoed like the warm Pacific waves, it moved in rhythm with the hula dancers. (A few decades later, early blues players would experiment with the same effects, using a knife or broken bottleneck to create bone-chilling moans.) Steel guitar was born, and with it a whole new voice and way of playing.

By the early part of the 20th century, a craze for Hawaiian music took root on the mainland and it lasted well into the 1950s, when New York's last big Hawaiian theme room closed. But though the fad ended, the music never stopped, evolving as it did into Nashville's pedal steel sound.

Weissenborn Hawaiian guitar, 1920s. The wood is Hawaiian koa, historically used to build the island's ocean-going canoes.

ALOHA

The Hawaiian guitar craze, which started at the turn of the 20th century and continued into the 1950s, had a lasting effect by bringing the guitar to center stage—which in turn helped set in motion the need for louder instruments. This Gibson HG-24 was marketed as a Hawaiian guitar to take advantage of the style's popularity. But its owner, Scott Chinery, pointed out a greater significance: the first large-body flattop with a dreadnought shape and a neck that joins the body at the 14th fret. It also sports four f-holes. John Dopyera clearly loved the Hawaiian guitar—his models span nearly 50 years, beginning in 1927.

Gibson HG-24, 1929

National Style 2 Hawaiian, 1927
Note the square neck, one of the key differences between
a "Hawaiian" guitar, to be played flat on the lap with
a steel, and a "Spanish" guitar, to be held on the knee
and fretted with your band.

WIZARD OF THE STRINGS

Roy Smeck, a Vaudeville
virtuoso on guitar, banjo,
harmonica, and ukulele,
dazzled audiences from
World War I on, not only
with his playing but with his
tricks—pretending to swallow
the harmonica, playing
behind his back, switching
instruments in mid-song.
Gibson introduced two
signature Smeck jumbos, the
Stage De Luxe (mahogany)
and the Radio Grande
(rosewood), both set up for
Hawaiian playing.

"Roy Smeck played steel guitar like a man whose taste had been surgically removed."
—Bob Brozman

Gibson Roy Smeck Stage De Luxe, 1935

ISLAND MAGIC

Love for that Hawaiian twang inspired guitar-makers and inventors throughout the first half of the 20th century—and even later. This stunning Dobro Hawaiian laptop with its Art Deco look (notice the f-holes along the lower fingerboard) is from 1936. Decades later, Dopyera would continue experimenting with his resonator design, creating this amplified one-of-a-kind Hawaiian model. The hinged circle at the top opens to a plush-lined storage compartment.

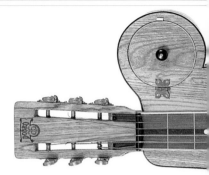

Dobro Hawaiian guitar, 1936

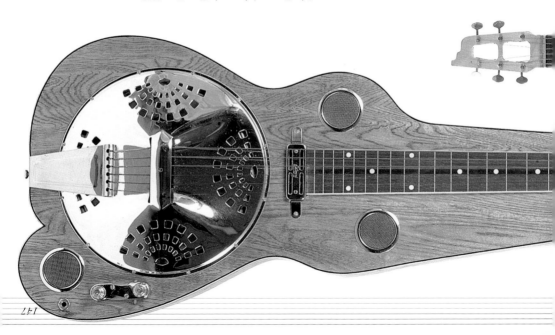

John Dopyera's lap-style Hawaiian, 1970s

OUT OF THE FRYING PAN . . .

It may be impossible to say who developed the first electric guitar, but Rickenbacker made history for being the first to manufacture and sell them, offering the legendary lap steel "Frying Pan" in 1932. What's especially interesting is that the Frying Pan is not just a museum piece but is still sought out by players for its unsurpassed tonal quality, created by the horseshoe pickup and heavy aluminum body.

*"Rickenbacher"
(original spelling)
Frying Pan, c. 1934
(front and back)*

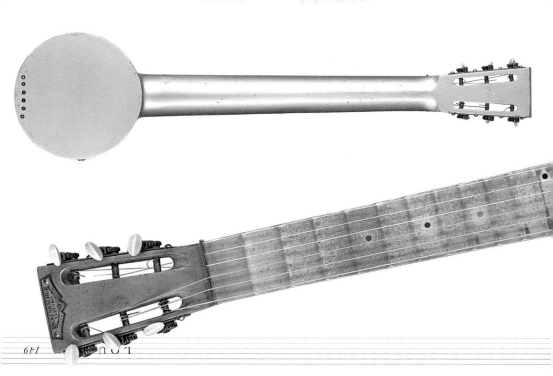

PLAYING HORSESHOES

Rickenbacker used its horseshoe pickup—an early design where the magnet wraps over the strings—to experiment with different types of electric guitars. This Electric-Spanish model is a visual conundrum: It reads like an archtop, but is in fact a flattop sporting fake f-holes in the upper bout and a slotted headstock decorated with mother-of-pearl. Note the single volume control. (Contemporary luthier Rick Turner reintroduces the horseshoe pickup in his Model T; see page 399.)

Rickenbacker Electric-Spanish, c. 1934

The split steel bar, in a U shape, is the pickup magnet.

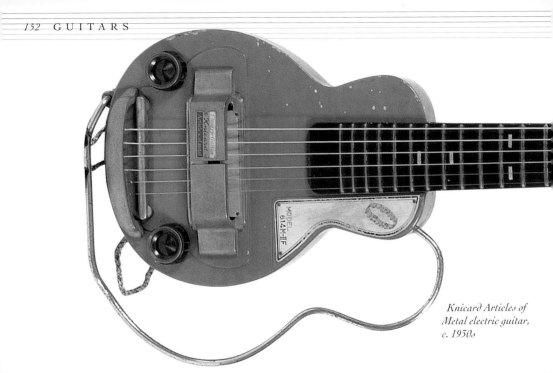

Knicard Articles of Metal electric guitar, c. 1930s

MISSING LINK?

Is it a "Hawaiian" guitar, to be played on the lap?
Or a Spanish guitar, to be played on the knee?
Everything about this guitar is mysterious—the
shape, the unexpected wire knee rest, even the
name. Good luck Googling "Knicard."

National electric archtop,
body by Regal, 1935

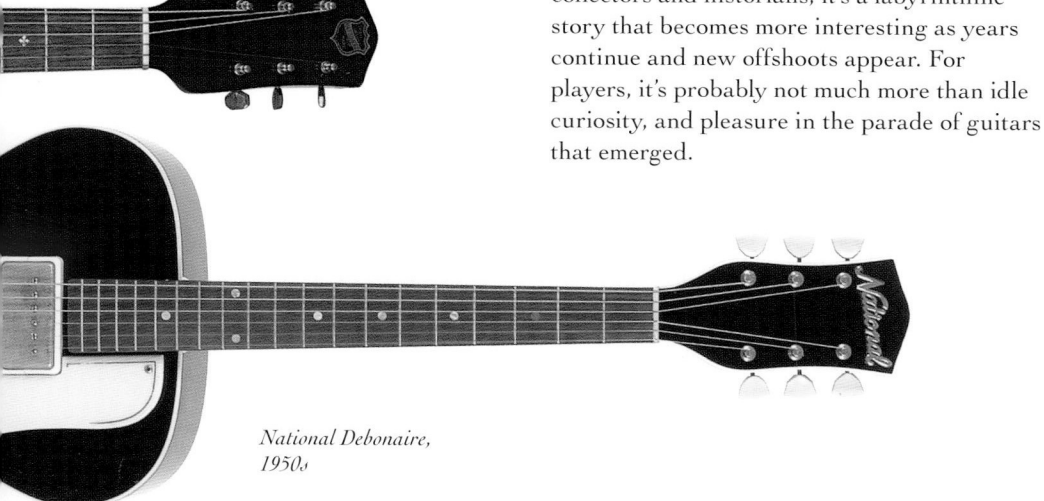

NATIONAL, DOBRO, VALCO . . . John Dopyera had his hands in all of these companies, and for collectors and historians, it's a labyrinthine story that becomes more interesting as years continue and new offshoots appear. For players, it's probably not much more than idle curiosity, and pleasure in the parade of guitars that emerged.

National Debonaire,
1950s

UNSUNG INVENTORS litter the guitar's history. One such is Paul H. Tutmarc, a Seattle-based musician, teacher, and tinkerer who, in 1930, was working on the promise of electrical amplification with a fellow tinkerer, Art Stimson. Stimson later disappeared to California, where he surreptitiously sold the rights to the pickup he and Tutmarc created to the Dopyera brothers. In 1933, Dobro released its first All-Electric. Note the engraved lightning bolts.

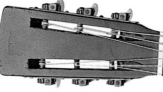

The Dobro All-Electric, 1933

SITTING UP

Like creatures coming out of the primordial ooze to stagger from four legs to two, Rickenbacker's early electric guitars developed along almost evolutionary lines. A few years after the Frying Pan, the Rickenbacker Electro Vibrola sprouted a motorized vibrato device in the tailpiece; a stand (not shown) also connected the instrument to an amp. The 1930s prototype here foreshadows the body shape of both the early Telecaster and Les Paul. And the black-and-white appointments are very sharp.

*Rickenbacker Electro
Vibrola, 1937*

*Early Rickenbacker
electric prototype, 1930s*

THE ROAD TO LES PAUL ...

began in 1935 with this R&D project to create an electric solid body. Scarcely resembling a guitar, it's essentially a concoction of brass sheets mounted on a brass ladder frame. But still the company's pride is evident in the shape of the peghead—classic Gibson.

*Gibson experimental
guitar, 1935
(front and back)*

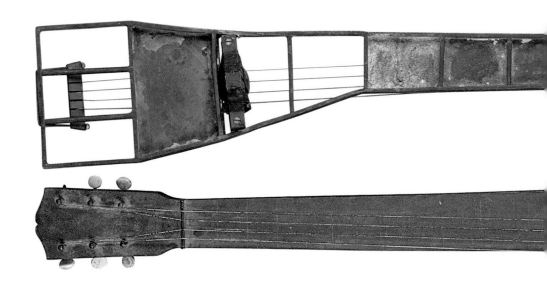

GREATS *Charlie Christian*

"**G**uitarmen, Wake Up and Pluck! Wire for Sound; Let 'Em Hear You Play." So proclaimed the jazz pioneer Charlie Christian in a manifesto he published in *Down Beat* magazine in 1939. Nourished on Lester Young, the tenor saxophonist, and Django Reinhardt, Christian revolutionized the guitar's role in jazz, and fundamentally all of pop, by being the first to explore the electric guitar's possibilities as a solo instrument. In Christian's hands, the guitar left the rhythm section and took center stage, as he fashioned gorgeous, swinging single-note lines, full of bluesy riffs and offbeat accents. His "audition" with Benny Goodman is the stuff of legend: During a break, John Hammond snuck him onto the stage, and the skeptical Goodman called for the band to play "Rose Room," a song he assumed the guitarist had never heard before. Christian took some 25 choruses in front of an audience hooting with amazement. Later, Christian helped forge bebop in Harlem nightclubs like Minton's, jamming after-hours with the likes of Dizzy Gillespie, Thelonious Monk, and Charlie Parker. Fortunately, recordings preserve some of his work. The guitarist died of tuberculosis at the age of 23.

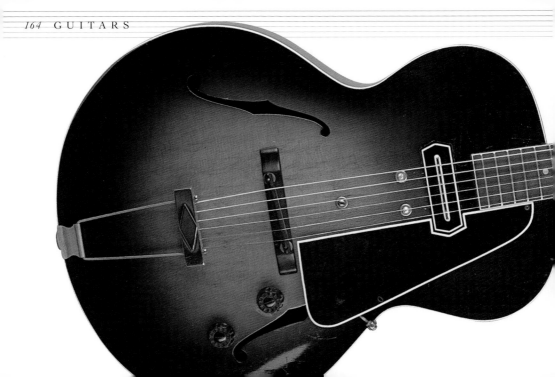

"A NEW LEASE ON LIFE" are words jazz guitarist Charlie Christian used in praising electrical amplification. Christian, the first musician to understand the full import of an amplified guitar, is forever linked with Gibson's first "Electric-Spanish" guitar, the ES-150. Many players still think it has the purest jazz tone of any electric guitar made. It is also the first electric guitar to prove itself commercially feasible.

Gibson ES-150, 1938,
known as the Charlie
Christian model

Vivi-Tone electric guitar, 1933 (front and back)

FAR AHEAD OF ITS TIME, this guitar created by Lloyd Loar and Vivi-Tone failed completely—like all the ill-timed Vivi-Tone instruments—and was all but forgotten. And yet, here it is, the world's first solid-body guitar—i.e., a guitar that derives its sound entirely from electricity. That's right: While it may look like a typical acoustic archtop, look again. It has no body, just a shapely front and a beam running down the back.

MASTER LOAR

The "Stradivarius of Kalamazoo," so called by Tom Wheeler in his lively and definitive history of American guitars, Lloyd Loar was either a musical prodigy with the mind of a scientist or a scientific pioneer with the ears of a master musician. Probably both.

An internationally known mandolinist by the age of 20, Loar approached the Gibson company with ideas for improving its mandolins. Gibson signed him on, and for the next five years, from 1919 to 1924, "Master Loar" blazed a path of greatness, introducing the iconic F-5 mandolin and the Master Line Master Tone series of instruments that included the groundbreaking L-5 guitar. Not a luthier per se, Loar wore multiple hats for the company as chief acoustic engineer, visionary of R&D, salesman, and trainer, obsessing over production and signing his name on the label of each instrument to verify its quality.

For Loar, everything revolved around tone, and his major contribution was the idea that each part of an instrument—tops, backs, tonebars, even the f-holes—could be "tuned" to create a more dynamic whole. Loar experimented with additional tone plates using a Virzi Tone Producer, a small spruce disk that was affixed to the underside of the soundboard to improve overtones. He also had designs for electric instruments, though this time Gibson rejected Loar's direction.

In 1933, Loar formed Vivi-Tone, where he explored his most offbeat ideas, including a full keyboard instrument that used tuned metal reeds instead of strings, and some of the most unusual guitars ever devised. Typically, Loar was ahead of his time: Vivi-Tone appeared just as the Depression gripped the country, and in 1938 the company ground to a halt.

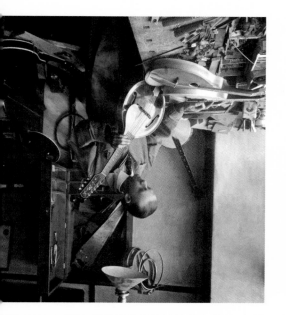

Lloyd Loar at his Gibson workbench, 1924

*Vivi-Tone Electro-Spanish guitar,
1934 (front and back)*

EQUALLY ODD, this acoustic-electric from Lloyd Loar shows how the brilliant mastermind behind the Gibson L-5 never stopped trying new ideas—even if they were of questionable merit, like the sound hole under the bridge; the f-holes in the back (considered a "secondary soundboard"); and the internal pickup accessed by a drawer in the side of the body—all present in this guitar.

AN AMAZING BEAST

In 1941, Les Paul created The Log. He'd previously experimented with a piece of railroad track and a plain 2×4. This time he made something that resembled a guitar, a 20-pound Frankenstein consisting of a 4×4 solid pine body, a Gibson neck, Larson fingerboard, split Epiphone "wings" to make it resemble a guitar, and pickups he created from the coils of an electric clock.

Les Paul's The Log,
1941

GIBSON PASSED on The Log, but 11 years later worked with Les Paul to unveil one of the all-time great American guitars, The Les Paul Model. The originals came in gold and had two "soapbar" pickups and a trapezoidal tailpiece that caused intonation problems. But what sustain! And what sales: 1,715 the first year, 2,245 the next, and so on.

Gibson Les Paul demo model, showing a before-and-after story of wood and construction. Date unknown.

Gibson Les Paul "Goldtop,"
c. 1955

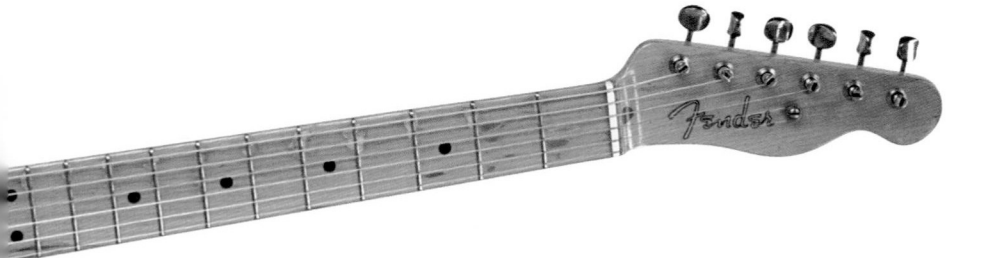

Fender "Nocaster,"
1951

END OF AN ERA

Throughout the first half of the 20th century, guitarists clamored to be heard. But probably no guitarist of the era could imagine just *how well* guitars would be heard once Leo Fender finished bolting the neck onto his first Tele-style instrument.

GREATS Chet Atkins, C.G.P.

In 1983, Chet Atkins awarded himself a "degree": C.G.P., Certified Guitar Player. No one would argue with that. A sensitive, asthmatic youth, "Mr. Guitar" developed his virtuosic thumb-and-three-fingers technique by listening to Merle Travis on the radio. He also drew inspiration from Django Reinhardt and jazz guitarist George Barnes, and though at first he came off as a neither-nor player—too sophisticated for country, too country for jazz—by his mid-20s, Chet Atkins was playing steadily with Homer & Jethro and The Carter Sisters and

was on his way to becoming probably *the* most recorded instrumentalist in history. More than any other individual, he validated Nashville's claim as Music City, USA, excelling as a solo artist, a session musician—his guitar can be heard on recordings by Hank Williams, Elvis Presley, The Everly Brothers, Kitty Wells—and a record producer who helped create the "Nashville Sound" and propelled the careers of dozens of country stars. At the heart of his legend, though, is his genius as a guitarist's guitarist: The clean lines, sparkling tone, tasteful arrangements, the swing, the humor, the variety—every note reveals a musician in masterful control of his instrument.

Gibson Flying V Prototype, 1957

THREE

American Icons

23 GUITARS THAT CHANGED HISTORY

he evolution of the guitar exploded in the 20th century. Guitars appeared in infinite variety. New musical styles demanded new tools, and new tools inspired new musical styles. Never-before-heard sounds seeped like rainwater into the consciousness of players, to emerge as never-before-heard music. Then someone would have a new idea—a different way to brace the guitar's top, a change to the pickup, to bend the strings—and a new instrument would be born.

Along the way certain guitars emerged where all the elements just fell into place, creating greatness. Think of them as icons. Some are revolutionary, most are evolutionary, all are stunningly successful. These instruments are embraced by musicians, copied by other makers, lusted after by collectors. Some, like the

Fender Stratocaster, spread their influence over whole spheres of music. Some appear years before their time, like the Gibson L-5. Others seem to arise out of the culture's clamor, like the Charvel Jackson Superstrat. Still others embody the virtue of being workmanlike, but stay relevant for decades. The Martin D-28 is your basic bassy, boomy, rosewood dreadnought; the Gibson J-45 a plain-Jane round-shouldered mahogany jumbo with the Gibson chunk—and seemingly everyone has played one or the other and usually both.

Guitar-makers profess to chase the ideal of versatility. A guitar that does it all is a seductive marketing promise. Of course, the opposite is really true. The great ones don't do it all; they just do it better.

GIBSON L-5
The Lloyd Loar Masterpiece

Introduced 1923
Model Shown 1924

① Some of the L-5's firsts include first f-hole archtop guitar,

② the first modern orchestra guitar,

③ and first guitar with a 14-fret neck to the body that had an adjustable truss rod.

④ One of the unexpected great players of an L-5 was Mother Maybelle Carter. She bought hers right after the Bristol Sessions in 1928.

Making its debut in 1923, the L-5 has such a résumé of "firsts" that even if it had fizzled as a viable guitar, it would still be a significant instrument. But it didn't fizzle. Its uncommon marriage of aesthetics and acoustics kept it as Gibson's top-of-the-line model for more than a decade, until the Super 400 arrived. And Gibson must have known it had something special on its hands, dubbing it "The Master Line Guitar L-5 Professional Special Grand Concert Model."

NATIONAL STYLE 2 "TRICONE"

"More Volume!"

Introduced 1928
Model Shown 1928

George Beauchamp was a Texas-born vaudeville performer who played Hawaiian guitar in his act, and like many players of the time, he had one wish: more volume! But he also had an idea—hook up a guitar with the kind of horn used in early phonographs. He took this idea to the Los Angeles–based inventor John Dopyera, who solved it by using a different part of phonograph amplification—the cone of a speaker. In 1927, Dopyera patented the three-cone configuration that would give birth to the iconic resonator guitar.

1 National offered a body made out of nickel-plated "German silver," an alloy of nickel, copper, and zinc.

2 The tri-cone has three spun-metal plates, or cones, in the body joined by a T-shaped bar that conveys the vibration from string to amplifying cones.

3 Style 2 features a simple rose design engraved on the body, front and back. The most expensive, Style 4, has a chrysanthemum pattern.

4 Nationals had either a round neck for Spanish playing or a square neck for Hawaiian playing. The most famous early adopter was the Hawaiian guitar hero Sol Hoopii.

GIBSON NICK LUCAS SPECIAL
The First Signature Guitar

Introduced 1928
Model Shown 1928

Today artist models and endorsements are a common strategy to connect customers with their favorite musicians. It all started when Gibson approached the most popular guitarist of the 1920s, "the Crooning Troubadour," Nick Lucas, who already played an L-1. Gibson may also have invented G.A.S. (Guitar Acquisition Syndrome) when it wrote the catalog copy: "Here is an instrument with a big, harplike tone, responsive to the lightest touch, balanced in every register. Crisp, sparkling treble and solid resonant bass that makes your whole being sway to its rhythmic pulsations. . . . an instrument by an artist, for an artist."

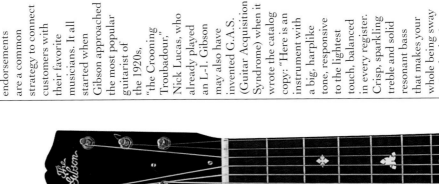

1 *Nick Lucas sold more than 80 million records, including hits like "Tiptoe Through the Tulips" and guitar-based tracks such as "Teasin' the Frets," but in a funny oversight, he is seen playing his L-1—not his Nick Lucas—on the inside label.*

2 *Among the finest flattops Gibson ever made, the Nick Lucas is distinguished by its extra-deep body. The best were made of maple.*

3 *This is a 12-fret model. Some had a neck that joined the body at the 13th fret.*

4 *Bob Dylan played a Nick Lucas as he was reaching wider fame around 1964–65.*

DOBRO
The Old Hound Dog Guitar

Introduced 1928
Model Shown 1970s

After inventing the National resophonic guitar, John Dopyera formed Dobro with the aim of making a single-cone resonator. But the Dobro's biggest innovation was to position the cone to face forward and suspend it by an eight-leg spider bridge. He also applied the resophonic designs to the violin, mandolin, ukulele, banjo, and even a massive stand-up bass. National responded by making single-cone instruments like the Style O, and after a lot of legal huffing and puffing, the companies merged.

1 This classic Dobro is from John Dopyera's personal collection.

2 Early Dobros had wooden bodies—the story was the company couldn't afford the tooling required to make metal-bodied instruments.

3 Though barely visible through the grill, the resonating cone sits in the body like a dish. An eight-legged bridge supports it and conducts the string's vibrations.

4 By 1935, the Dobro all but disappeared. Today it is most associated with bluegrass music, though players as diverse as Dickey Betts and Adrian Belew have used them.

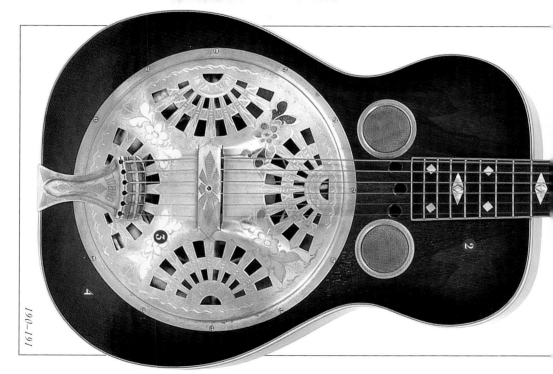

MARTIN OM-28
The Perfect Fingerstyle Instrument

Introduced 1929
Model Shown 1930

Time and again in the guitar's history, innovation is nudged along by a musician. The celebrated OM came about in 1929 when a banjo player named Perry Bechtel approached Martin about building a guitar that was easier for a banjo player to use, suggesting an instrument with a longer, narrower, 14-fret neck. Martin called it the OM for Orchestra Model, though it has since become the de facto design for a well-balanced guitar especially suited for fingerstyle playing.

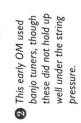

① The OM-28 is considered the first true modern steel-string guitar, making the 14-fret neck—one that attaches to the body at the 14th rather than 12th fret—the standard for steel-string acoustics. To achieve it originally, Martin shortened the upper bout.

② This early OM used banjo tuners, though these did not hold up well under the string pressure.

③ The OM headstock had no name, a small teardrop pickguard, slender V-shaped neck, and lighter bracing under the top.

④ The 14-fret neck became so successful that Martin discontinued the OM designation by 1934, though it uses it again today.

MARTIN D-18
Birth of the Banjo Killer

Introduced *1931*
Model Shown *1956*

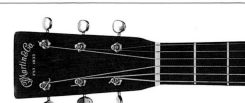

1 Martin's Style 18 indicates a mahogany body with spruce top and little decoration. Even the fretboard markers are plain dots.

2 The D-18 and (next page) D-28 share the same milestones, starting out as 12-fret guitars and evolving to 14-fret models in 1934.

3 After serving up nothing but natural-finish guitars for a century, in the 1930s Martin offered a few sunbursts, giving this plain-Jane D-18 a special look.

In the holy trinity of Martin pre-war dreadnoughts, the 18, 28, and 45, the D-18 holds the noble position of base instrument and is one of the company's best-selling models. It is unadorned to the point of severity—almost Shaker-like in its lack of appointments—but has a powerful, raucous voice. And with that mahogany body, nothing gets in the way of the pure delivery of tone, so dry and open it can hold its own in any mix. Bring on the banjos!

MARTIN D-28
The Power of Pure 'Bone

Introduced 1951
Model Shown 1941

In the 1910s, Martin Guitar made instruments for a number of different companies, including Boston-based music publisher Oliver Ditson. A New York store manager named Harry L. Hunt suggested the dreadnought design. Martin made them for a number of years, then the model vanished until the early 1950s, when they dusted off the original paper pattern to meet the same need: how to produce a powerful, versatile flattop with sufficient volume.

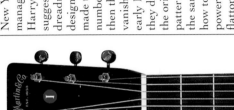

1 From the square headstock to the fine herringbone trim, this guitar is the very essence of what Martin is about.

2 This 1941 model is one of the last of the prewar herringbones. World War II would irrevocably force changes in materials and production, making prewar Martin dreadnoughts a rarity.

3 The D-28 started life as the 12-fret D-2. It has a rosewood body, an Adirondack spruce top, and was originally marketed as a "bass guitar" because of its big-bodied deep voice—which turned out to be perfectly suited to vocal accompaniment.

196-197

MARTIN D-45
Flagship of the Martin Line

Introduced 1933
Model Shown 1938

In 1933, at the height of his popularity, Gene Autry contacted Martin and requested a custom guitar, a 12-fret dreadnought with style 45 trim and his name writ large in abalone along the fretboard (see page 90). Martin then introduced the guitar as a 14-fret production model, the D-45, minus, of course, Gene Autry's name. Only 91 were built between 1933 and 1941, and they possessed extraordinary tone, quality, looks, and sheer presence—each is truly irreplaceable.

1 There's decoration everywhere. Even the tuners are engraved with the letter "M."

2 From the fretboard markers to the trim, D-45s glitter with abalone, a shellfish whose mother-of-pearl interior gives us the name "pearl." Martin used the "green heart" of the pearl for inlay.

3 Only nine D-45s were made in 1938; this sunburst model is so rare it may be unique in the prewar run of instruments.

4 Neil Young, hearing magic in old guitars, bought his D-45 in 1967. Today a prewar D-45 carries an astronomical price tag.

GIBSON SUPER 400
The Aristocrat of Archtops

Introduced 1934
Model Shown 1935

A decade after the milestone L-5, Gibson achieved the pinnacle of its archtop offerings with the Super 400. The Super 400's 1934 debut was spectacular: Here was an instrument that was simply bigger, bolder, richer—a massive 18" jazz masterpiece that exuded luxury from peghead to tailpiece. It was also quite an act of confidence on Gibson's part, introducing a $400 instrument during the very depths of the Depression. (Gibson's next-priciest guitar was the $275 L-5.) By 1940, Gibson widened the upper bout, offered a premier cutaway, and shifted from X-bracing to a more sonically open parallel bracing.

1. The signs of luxury begin at the top, with the slash diamond design on the peghead, and continue down the fretboard, with its slash block fret markers.

2. Another sign of Gibson luxury—the parenthesis point at the end of the fretboard.

3. Gibson used a unique layering technique to achieve the marbleized-tortoise look of the pickguard. All the metal parts are gold-plated; seven layers of binding outline the body.

4. The name "Super 400" is engraved on the tailpiece. Gibson often showed the instrument with a decorative ribbon tied around its waist.

D'ANGELICO NEW YORKER
The Essence of Jazz-Age Manhattan

Introduced 1936
Model Shown 1955

Artists learn from other artists. John D'Angelico learned from Lloyd Loar and based his earlier guitars on the Gibson L-5. Gradually, befitting the master he became, D'Angelico soon developed his own extraordinary styles and designs. He offered four basic models, with the 18" X-braced New Yorker at the top of the line. Along with its size, it is distinguished by its cosmetic appointments—the split block inlays, additional layers of binding, and the very cool New Yorker inlay. With its powerful, balanced, smooth tone, this is the very epitome of a jazz orchestra archtop guitar.

1 A story is told of how D'Angelico used to stare out of his shop window at the Chrysler Building, finding inspiration for the Art Deco elements in his guitars. The New Yorker inlay was supposedly patterned after the Empire State Building.

2 This is a very rare left-handed model.

3 The setbacks of a New York skyscraper are everywhere in the design: tailpiece, pickguard, truss rod cover, even the gold Grover Imperial tuners.

4 Because each was built by hand and many were commissioned by musicians, D'Angelico guitars never stopped evolving.

GIBSON SJ-200
"King of the Flattop Guitars"

Introduced 1957
Model Shown 1959

1 Everything about the SJ-200 is bigger and fancier, starting with the oversized, decorated pickguard and pearl markers on the fretboard.

2 Note the distinctive mustache bridge shaped like cattle horns.

3 Whitley suggested the large, deep body and a longer scale length; the narrow waist was borrowed from the then-enlarged L-5. Postwar models like this one are made of maple.

4 A powerful lineup of players have used the SJ-200 over the years, from Mance Liscomb to Bob Dylan to the Reverend Gary Davis to Keith Richards, Emmylou Harris, and The Edge.

Martin had Gene Autry. Gibson, which lagged for several years in the production of big flattops, found its own cowboy star/guitar designer in a man named Ray Whitley. While at a rodeo show at Madison Square Garden, Whitley hooked up with a Gibson man named Ray Hart and suggested the company build a real country music guitar. Gibson invited Whitley to its plant at Kalamazoo for more discussion, and that very day Gibson engineers began designing a guitar based on Whitley's ideas—a big, gutsy, flamboyant showpiece that became known as the Super Jumbo 200.

GIBSON J-45
The Gibson That's Always Good Enough

Introduced 1942
Model Shown 1966

1 Sunburst was Gibson's regular finish, critical to the World War II–era J-45, because it could hide flaws in the wood available during wartime.

2 A J-45 with a natural finish is designated a J-50. The two are often referred to interchangeably.

3 The specs are Gibson flattop basics: wide mahogany body, spruce top with scalloped X-bracing, 24.75" scale.

4 The J-45 (and J-50) roster of players includes folk blues artists like Mississippi John Hurt, Lightnin' Hopkins, and the Reverend Robert Wilkins as well as Jeff Tweedy, Aimee Mann, and Bruce Springsteen.

Martin had the square-shouldered dreadnought, Gibson the round-shouldered jumbo. Lots and lots of jumbos: the mythical Advanced Jumbo, the round-bottomed Super Jumbos, the prewar J-35, and the rare J-55, with its fingerboard of "genuine polished coffeewood." Then in 1942, Gibson introduced one of those special models where everything comes together: the workaday J-45. With its warm, sweet tone, superb playability, and outstanding value—listed originally at $45, hence the designation—the J-45 is among Gibson's most popular and successful guitars.

GIBSON ES-175
Striking the Right Balance

Introduced *1949*

Model Shown *1960*

Gibson has made dozens and dozens of electric guitars since the ES-150. In fact, dozens of electric hollow-body jazz guitars. But in 1949 it issued a new model—the ES-175—that found just the right combination of quality and value, giving it the distinction of being the most long-lived postwar electric and Gibson's first successful electric. With its relatively small body made of pressed, laminated maple/basswood, it has a bright cutting tone, making it attractive to more than just jazz players.

1 *Along with the introduction of electric-only instruments like the ES-175, Gibson also began offering cutaways—after all, before amplification, those upper treble notes would have been lost anyway.*

2 *By 1957, the 175 came fitted with humbuckers. Gibson also made an ES-175D, with two pickups—the "D" stands for "double."*

3 *A fancy tailpiece with zigzag rods shows up around the same time as the humbuckers.*

4 *A list of ES-175 players reads like a jazz hall of fame—Joe Pass, Jim Hall, Herb Ellis, Pat Metheny. Another fan is Steve Howe of Yes.*

FENDER BROADCASTER
The Most Important Electric Guitar Ever Made

Introduced 1950
Model Shown 1950

Like Henry Ford before him, Leo Fender changed everything by applying mass-production techniques to the manufacture of guitars—and creating a function-follows-form masterpiece that made the solid-body electric guitar a reality. And in the case of the Broadcaster/Telecaster—the name was changed to Telecaster in the late '50s to avoid a possible trademark conflict with Gretsch—it's a masterpiece that continues to shine more than 50 years later. It's stripped-down, unpretentious, virtually indestructible, and easy to play, and it serves up that legendary twang.

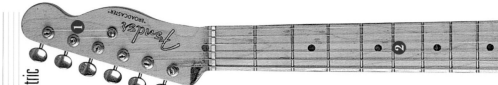

❶ Instruments with just the word Fender on the headstock are now known as "Nocasters."

❷ The ingredients couldn't be simpler: hard rock-maple neck, ash body, adjustable truss rod, all for $170.

❸ Two single-coil pickups introduced the clean, bright Fender sound, developed out of Leo Fender's love of the lap steel guitar and its Hawaiian twang.

❹ The Broadcaster/ Telecaster started out as a cowboy guitar but has since been played by James Burton, Muddy Waters, Roy Buchanan, and Albert Lee.

LES PAUL
The Mythological 'Burst

Introduced 1952
Model Shown 1959

By 1950, change was in the air, and Gibson needed to make a solid-body electric guitar. But they didn't want it to be just another "plank" (i.e., Fender Telecaster). Gibson's solution: a rich-looking, carved-top single-cutaway made out of a maple and mahogany sandwich. They brought the prototype to Les Paul, who suggested they paint it gold. To reinvigorate sales, in the late '50s, Gibson changed to a traditional cherry sunburst and replaced the pickups with the new humbuckers. These original "bursts" exude a musicality, a growl, a soul that's never been duplicated.

1 Gibson launched its solid-body by teaming up with Les Paul.

2 From mid-1957 until 1962, Les Paul humbuckers were stickered PATENT APPLIED FOR, or PAF, and some players (and collectors) believe they have an almost mystical quality.

3 The body is mahogany with a maple "cap." The wood is bookmatched to create symmetrical patterns under the finish.

4 Mike Bloomfield, Eric Clapton, and Jimmy Page discovered a deep, throaty sound in the Les Paul, perfect for their blues-based rock.

FENDER STRATOCASTER
Lightning Strikes Twice

Introduced 1954
Model Shown 1954

1 The perfect six-on-a-side peghead was designed in response to the minimal Telecaster style.

2 Everything is new: Two cutaways, the beveled body, an unheard-of three pickups with selector switch, adjustable bridge for each string (concealed beneath the bridge cover), protected output jack, and angled lead pickup for better treble response.

3 The vibrato unit, or "whammy bar," was so revolutionary that it took a decade, when Jimi Hendrix came along, to be fully explored.

4 Hendrix, Clapton, George Harrison, The Edge, Buddy Holly, Buddy Guy, Stevie Ray Vaughan—who hasn't played a Strat?

Guitarists loved the Telecaster, but with reservations: It was perhaps too plain vanilla. And the heavy, blocky body was hard on the ribs. So Leo Fender listened, and with the help of two players—Freddy Tavares and Bill Carson—created a second masterpiece. Unveiled in 1954, the Stratocaster is probably the most played, most popular, most copied electric guitar ever. It arrived as if out of the future. Sleek, curvy, and contoured, it was a love-it-or-hate-it object that seemed more the product of a car designer than a guitar-maker. But musicians knew, and over time virtually every electric guitarist played one.

GRETSCH CHET ATKINS COUNTRY GENTLEMAN

Rockabilly Twang from the Heart of Brooklyn

Introduced 1957
Model Shown 1960s

Gretsch had built musical instruments in its various Brooklyn shops since 1883. But the company didn't find real fame and fortune until the mid-1950s, when it introduced its highly distinctive electric guitars. With their bluesy twang, flashy design, and wild colors—they were the first manufacturer to amp up the palette, with colors like Cadillac Green and Flagstaff Sunset.

Gretsch attracted a series of musicians, including Chet Atkins, who gave his name to several models he helped design. When George Harrison played a Country Gentleman on television, it sent the company into orbit.

1 *The design of the Country Gent is fairly restrained, for Gretsch, with a traditional headstock, neoclassic "thumbprint" fret markers, walnut stain—and the famous fake F-hole markers.*

2 *Gretsch liked to put a lot of gadgets at the player's disposal, including a Bigsby vibrato, mute knobs, standby switch, and master volume knob.*

3 *In addition to George Harrison and Chet Atkins, famous Gretsch players include Elvis, Duane Eddy, Brian Setzer, Pete Townshend, and Mike Nesmith—Gretsch offered a Monkees signature guitar in 1966.*

The year 1958 saw not only the introduction of Gibson's flamboyant but faltering "Modernistic" line of guitars but also the thin-line design heralded by the ES-335. Considered one of the greatest milestones in electric guitar design, the 335 is a double-cutaway that marries the warmth of a hollow-body jazz guitar with the sustain of a solid-body electric. The innovation lies in the use of a solid maple block that runs through the middle of the "wonder-thin" body and eliminates the feedback problem common to hollow-body guitars played at high volume. Innumerable variations followed, including a stereo version—the ES-345—in 1959.

GIBSON ES-335
The "Wonder-Thin" Wunderkind

Introduced 1958
Model Shown 1959

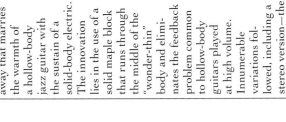

1. Afficionados call the pre-1962 335s "dot necks" because of the fret markers. In 1962, the dots were changed to blocks.

2. Early 335s were fitted for stop-tailpieces; some also had Bigsby vibratos. This was changed to a trapeze tailpiece in 1964, giving it more the feel of a true jazz guitar.

3. ES-335s were originally available in sunburst and natural; the famous cherry-red was introduced in 1960.

4. B.B. King's Lucille is the most famous 335 guitar. Others who played it include Chuck Berry, Eric Clapton, and Larry Carlton.

FLYING V
Gibson Tries on a New Look

Introduced 1958
Model Shown 1957 prototype

Challenged in the 1950s by the radical upstart Fender, Gibson decided it needed to shake things up. Designers generated dozens of new ideas to feed into the rock 'n' roll–inspired craze for guitars. Three were announced as part of a new "Modernistic" line, two were produced, and only one survived to become recognized as a classic, the arrow-shaped Flying V. After the guitar's introduction in 1958, dealers took them off the floor, where they weren't selling, and hung them in the window to attract attention. Somehow Cadillac could sell a car with fins, but Gibson had to wait another decade before the V started to fly.

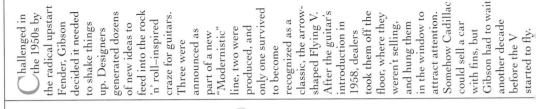

1 The original Modernistics—Flying V, Explorer, and the mysterious Moderne—were made of korina, a trade name for African limba wood.

2 This prototype of the Flying V has a black pickguard and input jack plate, but most original models had white trim.

3 Gibson shipped only 98 Flying Vs in the 1950s, making original models very rare and collectible. Flying V reissues started showing up in 1967, and the model has attracted a roster of important players, including Albert King, Jimi Hendrix, and Marc Bolan.

GIBSON SG
Schooled in Rock

*Introduced 1961
Model Shown 1961*

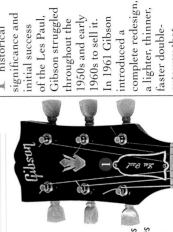

For all of the historical significance and initial success of the Les Paul, Gibson struggled throughout the 1950s and early 1960s to sell it. In 1961 Gibson introduced a complete redesign, a lighter, thinner, faster double-cutaway that bore the Les Paul name but was soon designated the SG (standing, somewhat prosaically, for Solid Guitar). Les Paul himself hated it, but rock guitarists loved it, and it attracted a veritable hall of fame of fans.

1 With Paul's name still on the headstock, transition models are known as Les Paul/SG models.

2 "A guy could kill himself on those sharp horns," Les Paul said when he first saw one. "The neck was too skinny . . . and there wasn't enough wood. So I called Gibson and told them to take my name off the thing."

3 The SG employed a sideways vibrato mounted on the front under the large cover plate.

4 Famous SG players include Eric Clapton, Tommy Iommi, Angus Young, Pete Townshend, and Frank Zappa.

RICKENBACKER 360/12
That Jingle Jangle Chiming

Introduced 1964
Model Shown 1960s

It's "the most famous chord in all of rock & roll" said *Rolling Stone* about the jarring, jangling blast George Harrison played on his Rickenbacker at the opening of "A Hard Day's Night." It's also one of the most famous sounds—the Rickenbacker 12-string chime that gave folk-rock its sonic personality on The Byrds' recording of "Mr. Tambourine Man." It happened in February 1964, when Rickenbacker was displaying an experimental 360/12 at the Savoy Hilton Hotel to show The Beatles as they prepared to invade America. George Harrison walked away with it. And Rickenbacker made history again—30 years after the Frying Pan.

1. Rickenbacker brilliantly solved the balance problems inherent in 12-string headstocks by keeping six tuners where they were and adding a modified slot design with keys facing backward.

2. Unique flourishes abound, including the split chrome "toaster top" pickups and the two-tiered pickguard, the upper half raised to use as a finger-rest.

3. At the same time as George picked up the experimental 360/12, Rickenbacker gave John Lennon a brand-new replacement for his much-used 325. Other Rickenbacker players are Roger McGuinn and Peter Buck of REM.

PRS "SANTANA"

"The Stradivarius of the Electric Guitar"

Introduced *1980*
Model Shown *1980*

1 PRS guitars use a 25"-scale—midway between Fender and Gibson—and in-house designed and wound pickups.

2 The famous bird markers, used on higher-end models, are inspired by a guidebook belonging to Smith's mother, a bird-watcher.

3 Beautiful, popping wood grain is a PRS signature. The first wood Smith used was curly maple from the drawer-fronts of a friend's dresser.

4 Santana is the official endorser, but PRS guitars are played by a huge roster of rock, country, and even jazz players, including Ted Nugent, Al DiMeola, Joe Walsh, and Dickey Betts.

More evolutionary than revolutionary, Paul Reed Smith found the middle way between Gibson and Fender to create PRS, one of the most respected and successful electric guitar makers in America. A sublime craftsman with a musician's instincts, he built one of his earliest guitars for idol Carlos Santana in 1980. Santana was so impressed that he called the guitar "an act of God." How could this nobody working out of a tiny shop in Annapolis, Maryland, create such an amazing instrument? It took two more guitars before Santana acknowledged these acts of God were the acts of a man creating a new American classic.

JACKSON/CHARVEL RANDY RHOADS
Birth of the Super-Strat

Introduced *1985*
Model Shown *1985*

Which comes first, the guitar or the music? In the case of an L-5, for example, it took years for the music to catch up. But here Jackson/Charvel were hurrying to fulfill the needs of hotshot guitarists who had outgrown the Gibsons and Fenders. Working with supershredders like Eddie Van Halen and Randy Rhoads, they created stripped-down, speeded-up, radical "super-Strats," perfect machine-gun-like guitars with aggressive looks and a fast, fat tone that served the needs of 1980s heavy-duty rock.

1 *Wayne Charvel had a guitar repair shop in California; guitarist Grover Jackson joined him, then bought the company in 1978. They produced guitars under both names.*

2 *The "super-Strat" offered more frets for extra pitch range, hotter pickups to capture the treble, flattened fingerboards, high-quality vibrato, funky graphics.*

3 *The first "Jackson" came out in 1983, designed in collaboration with guitarist Randy Rhoads, who wanted a Flying V but "more shark-finny."*

Jose Ramirez I,
1899

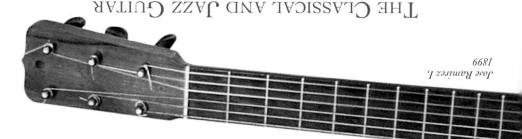

Uptown, Long-Haired, and Over-the-Top

FOUR

We may not want to believe it, but it's true: Not all guitar music is loud, or bluesy, or replicable with three chords. There are scales beyond the pentatonic, and players who've never even seen tablature. Ever the chameleon, the guitar is just as capable as any instrument of dressing in black tie and appearing at Carnegie Hall. Of behaving well in polite company, or staying in the background with tight, tasteful comping. This is the guitar's mature, respectable side. The guitar you learn to play by attending a conservatory or a college program, the guitar that is the province of what's commonly known as the "professional musician." The guitar whose peghead you would never, in a million years, use as a cigarette holder. (See Eric Clapton's "Brownie," page 341.)

The classical guitar. The jazz guitar. The grown-up guitar.

Contemporary classical guitar as a concert and recital form is in large part the creation of one individual, Andrés Segovia. The repertoire is limited, a mixture of early music for lute and *vihuela* and harpsichord,

Michael Greenfield C3 classical guitar, 2000s

of Bach pieces for solo violin and cello, of 19th-century Spanish composers like Fernando Sor and Francisco Tárrega, and of modern compositions often inspired by or commissioned by Segovia and the masters who followed him, Julian Bream and John Williams, Christopher Parkening and Sharon Isbin.

Far more than any other type of guitarist, the classical musician is dependent on the quality of his instrument. There he or she is, alone on stage, with nothing between fingers and audience but the barest essentials—strings and wood—out of which is to be coaxed music that will move a hall full of strangers. Nylon strings produce less tension, so the whole instrument is lighter and more responsive than its cousin, the steel-string flattop: no need for a metal truss rod in the neck, no need to worry as much about the thinness of the top, no need for the heavier cross-braces. Classical guitar rarely calls for strumming, and never a pick; the attack is all in the fingers. The best guitars are capable of an extraordinary range of tone and feeling:

Gaetano Guadagnini, 1838

finding one becomes a quest for the holy grail, but without the insanity that's infected the vintage and collectors' markets for nonclassical guitars. (Hendrix played it? Tack two or three zeros to the end of the price.)

Torres set the paradigm, and the instruments that followed tell a tale of millimeters, with change found in the most subtle variations of body shape, strut placement, top thicknesses, and string length. The history even reads like an old-fashioned patriarchy: Torres begat the Ramirez brothers who begat Hauser and so on. To the untrained eye, five, seven, even ten decades of classical guitars will look remarkably the same. But then think of them like bottles of wine: It's all about what's inside, with a nod to the label.

D'Aquisto Centura DeLuxe, 1994

Manuel Ramirez proved this in a creative demonstration. Ramirez, one of the most important of all Spanish builders (he built the guitar that a young Segovia played while rising to international acclaim), came to possess two of Torres's labels. Chafing under the mantle of "Torres's heir"—he considered himself the great man's equal—he built two Torres-like guitars and affixed the labels to the insides. In a classical version of *Punk'd*, Ramirez then invited accomplished players to judge the guitars. They all raved that these were the best Torres guitars they'd ever played. At which point Ramirez peeled off the Torres labels to reveal his own name underneath.

Segovia loved the Ramirez guitar so much that as he took it around the world with him, he invited other luthiers to measure it, study it, and try to duplicate it. A German luthier named Hermann Hauser found it to be a revelation. For the next 13 years, he painstakingly worked on perfecting the Spanish style until he created an instrument that Segovia found acceptable. This Hauser guitar became as famous and entwined with Segovia as the Ramirez. Julian Bream had a chance to play the Hauser, observing that it was "so delicate that you almost feel it will explode if you play a loud chord," and went on to add: "In fact, the greatest guitar that I ever played was Segovia's Hauser."

Still, innovations do appear, even if what's most different is not visible to the eye. Australian luthier Greg Smallman replaced traditional fan braces with a lattice system of balsa wood reinforced with carbon fiber, making the tops responsive to the lightest touch and solving the inherent problem of increasing volume without sacrificing tone; drive an acoustic guitar hard, and those lovely notes turn into plonks and thwacks. German maker Matthias Dammann developed a top that's like a sandwich: two slices of spruce or cedar with a honeycomb lattice between them. And there is Thomas Humphrey's Millennium concept, which features a sloped top, negative neck angle, and a raised fretboard, all designed to produce greater power as well as provide easier access to the upper frets. No surprise, perhaps, that the original idea for such a radical change came to Humphrey in a dream.

Curiously, while the classical guitar evolved out of what was essentially a folk instrument, the jazz, or archtop, guitar evolved out of the most highbrow of classical instruments, the violin. And even though classical players need a guitar that will respond to the slightest wiggle of their pinky, jazz guitarists can do just fine with something a tad less refined—an instrument that's going to punch out rhythm, sing a solo just like the horns, and look sharp on stage, but doesn't require that last exacting 1 percent difference between great and perfect. A great archtop can even be made in a factory. Just ask the myriad Gibson players.

Gibson invented the archtop guitar, and soon after, it and other companies and luthiers took the essential design to extraordinary heights of craftsmanship. Gibson's archtop "L" series not only spawned the milestone L-5 and its siblings, but it evolved into the magnificent (our word) Super (their word) 400. Meanwhile, back in New York, a banjo company founded by a Greek-born violin-maker transformed itself into a guitar manufacturer named Epiphone. Though contemporary players will know Epiphone as a low-end Gibson, from the 1930s through the mid-1950s, the "House of Stathopoulos" made a potent series of archtops with fanciful vine inlays and names that bestowed a sense

Epiphone Emperor Regent, c. 1954

of grandeur on the owner: Emperor, Zephyr, Broadway, Triumph, Royal, Ritz. And for a while, even Martin dipped its toe into the archtop world.

Individual archtop builders competed as well for the working guitarist. Up in Boston, from the 1930s to the early '50s, Elmer Stromberg and his father, Charles, hand-built approximately 640 archtop guitars, some of them colossal 19" beauties for the big-band guitarist looking to send acoustic cannonballs through the mix of horns, drums, piano, and more.

And then there was John D'Angelico. An apprentice violin-maker who went on to train with his grand-uncle, Raphael Ciani, a maker of fine Italian-style mandolins and flattop guitars, this old-school artisan opened a workshop on Kenmare Street, in Manhattan's Lower East Side, where he hand-carved some of the most beautiful archtops ever made. D'Angelicos, of which 1,164 were built, came in four flavors: the A, the B, the Excel, and—the crème de la crème—the New Yorker. Since every jazz artist passed through New York sooner or later, it was easy for musicians to drop in and work with D'Angelico personally, conferring on woods, sizes, shape of the neck, and other custom features. The D'Angelico, the Chrysler Building of guitars, epitomized the era of sophisticated big-city jazz. They are knowing, classy, with the right amount of flash to stand out from the crowd. And their voice is just as moneyed and uptown: smooth, sweet, articulate, and balanced.

Amplification just about killed these high-end archtops. But through the work of D'Angelico's genius apprentice, Jimmy D'Aquisto—who, with a few other builders like Bob Benedetto, carried the archtop torch over the dark period when everyone wanted to play a Strat—the form never disappeared. Today it is stronger than ever, presenting its unique challenges to new generations of luthiers.

Ironically, there may be more talented builders out there than there are talented players—or talented listeners. It's one thing to treat yourself to a high-end Martin for two or three thousand bucks and strum "Knockin' on Heaven's Door." You can close your eyes and feel like a bona fide guitar player. Not so easy to justify spending three to five times that on a hand-carved archtop and fumble through a chord-solo of "All the Things You Are."

Welcome to the world of not-three-chords.

FAMOUS MAKER

Stradivarius is synonymous today with the very highest quality, and in most people's minds conjures up a violin—with a multimillion dollar price tag. But in addition to the violins, cellos, and violas that he perfected, Antonio Stradivari of Cremona, Italy, made guitars, although only two authenticated instruments are known to survive.

The Ashmolean Stradivarius, c. 1700, a five-course guitar. Note the lack of adornment, frets extending on the top, and placement of the bridge, which gives it a very long scale length.

FAMOUS PLAYERS

Talk about mojo: This unimposing instrument was owned, played, and signed by two of the great geniuses of music: Niccolo Paganini and Hector Berlioz. They signed it together, when Paganini gave it to Berlioz, as a testament to both their friendship and their love of the guitar.

Grobert 6-string guitar, c. 1820s

The first rock star? Paganini mesmerized audiences with both his playing and his look.

GREATS *Niccolò Paganini*

Call him the superstar of his day. The legendary violin virtuoso would arrive fashionably late at the concert hall, in a black coach drawn by black horses, completely dressed in black, with long black hair and a pale white face, and proceed to astonish the audience with his playing. No one had ever heard anything like him before. And like Robert Johnson, he was so preternaturally gifted that rumors had Paganini selling his soul to the devil in return for his violin chops. But the fact is Paganini was equally brilliant on the guitar, with listeners claiming they couldn't tell which he played better. Today, scientists speculate that he suffered from Ehlers-Danos Syndrome, which produces hypermobile joints, allowing his long, rubbery fingers to reach everywhere on the fretboard. But there's another explanation, one that every aspiring rock 'n' roller will identify with: that the young Paganini woodshedded "in absolute retirement at the château of a lady of high rank, devoting much time to the study of the guitar, the lady's favorite instrument."

THE HISTORY OF THE GUITAR

C arved into a tile from ancient Babylonia is a man in a position familiar to anyone who's ever seen a guitarist working on a chord change. Disregard, for a moment, the details: that the individual is almost certainly a priest, is naked as ritual requires, and is holding the body of the instrument against his chest rather than on his knee. Instead, consider only the person's physical attitude. It's barely a stretch to imagine this Babylonian transported to a bench in the middle of Washington Square Park on a warm afternoon, so instantly recognizable is the image. He also has an animal at his side. Could it be Jim Jackson's "Old Dog Blue"?

Technically, he's not playing "the guitar." Andrés Segovia gave the guitar a fanciful mythic origin: "During Apollo's rape of Daphne, she was changed into a laurel tree, and from that sacred wood the guitar was born." In fact, the guitar as a distinct entity did not exist until the 15th century. There were many stringed, fretted instruments; the one depicted in the tile was probably a type of tanbur, a raspy-sounding instrument with a long tradition of use in sacred music. The ancient Greeks played a *kithara*, which, though the name sounds vaguely guitarlike, was a neckless instrument closer to the harp. Out of the Arabic world in the 9th century came the *'ud*, a round-backed stringed instrument with a short neck. The Moors brought it with them when they invaded southern Spain. Other Medieval instruments with guitar-sounding names—*guitarra, chitarra, guiterne, gittern*—were types of lutes (and possibly future mandolins). With their intricate, bowl-shaped bodies made out of wooden ribs, lutes were the direct descendent of the *'ud*, and, voiced to play newly written polyphonic music, became the favored solo instrument of Renaissance Europe.

Another important guitar forebear was the *vihuela*, a flat-bodied, pinch-waisted

Woodcut of Orpheus playing the vihuela, *c. 1550s*

Spanish instrument that came in three styles: to be bowed, played with a feather quill, or plucked with the fingers. It was this last version, the *vihuela de mano*, with its six "courses" of strings, that captured the Spanish imagination while serious music-makers in the rest of Europe were focused on the lute. (Early guitars and guitarlike instruments were strung with pairs of strings called courses, either tuned in unison or in octaves.) Whether the father of the guitar or just a highbrow cousin, the *vihuela* and the guitar were discussed interchangeably in the literature of the day. Also sometimes unflatteringly. One contemporary writer dismissed the original four-course guitar as nothing more than a "*vihuela* shorn of its first and sixth strings." Only one *vihuela* is known to have survived, though its prominence is indisputable given the amount of music written for it. And given the types of music that could be played on the *vihuela*, including fantasias, pavanes (a slow, courtly dance), love songs, and ballads, it is no surprise that many mourned the *vihuela*'s passing at the hands of the upstart, and much less couth, guitar.

Spanish Five-course guitar, 18th C., showing the elaborate ornamentation of the Baroque period

What of those first "four-course" guitars? Even with doubling up the gut strings, early guitars had little bass presence. They were most suited to accompanying a singer or, at best, could be used to pluck out a simple dance melody. Few composers took the four-course guitar seriously. Alonso Mudarra published six pieces in Seville in 1546, but he was the exception, and the rest of the province viewed the guitar as a denizen of taverns and barbershops, belonging in the hands of uneducated troubadours and roustabouts, romantics and country folk.

Yes, exactly the point! Already the guitar was starting to work its mysterious, mercurial charm, already it was reaching for something vital, almost elemental, that other instruments could never quite touch. Its very restrictions, in fact, contributed to its rising popularity. Unable to handle complex lute pieces, the guitar encouraged the free-spirited player to strum noisy chords. And while the Spanish musical elite looked down its nose at this humble homegrown instrument, the rest of Europe took notice. France's King Henry II invited several guitarists to his court. By 1570, guitar music was published in London. And the guitar also traveled beyond Europe's borders: As early as 1568, native Americans, having come into contact with Spanish conquistadores, were making guitars and *vihuelas*.

As the four-course guitar worked its way through Europe, someone thought to add on another set of strings, giving birth to the five-course guitar. Beautiful examples still exist, including two by the legendary violin-maker Antonio Stradivari. Much about the culture of the five-course guitar will be familiar to the contemporary player. The music is written in tablature, the simplified musical notation that indicates by numbers, letters, or diagrams where the player should place his fingers. The tuning is déjà vu all over again: *a/a-d/d'-g/g-b/b-e'*. There are even "fake books" that use a system of indicating chord sequences called *alfabeto*. Italians in particular adopted the guitar, aristocrats included. And a handful of virtuosos spread the music. An Italian player

Spanish 5-course guitar, 17th century, a study in ebony and ivory

Five-course guitar from Bordeaux, 17th century

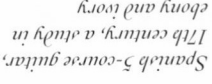

named Francesco Corbetta, the Segovia of his day, gave the guitar bug to two members of the nobility: Louis XIV of France and England's Charles II.

Still, the guitar as we know it needed almost another century of transition. The Neopolitan *chitarra battente,* developed circa 1740 for use in strummed *albafeto* accompaniment, introduced the innovation of metal strings: They sound louder (ah, the eternal quest for volume) and hold their pitch better (with gut strings prone to softening on hot summer days, tuning could literally melt away). Metal strings also required metal frets: Previously frets were tied-on pieces of gut, unable to withstand the pressing down of a sharp metal string.

Another key, if logical, step was the change from five courses of strings to six courses. This added a true bass tone with the low E. Along the way, bodies grew larger for a richer, more romantic voice. A fingerboard was added to the neck, which joined the body at the 12th fret, and the sound holes were kept open; previously, they were filled with decorative rings of parchment cut into rosettes and lacy patterns. Then, six courses turned into just six strings, and the guitar found itself attracting ever more serious composers.

Chitarra
battente,
*c. 1740, with
bowl back*

Anyone who plays classical guitar or dabbles in it to practice sight reading will recognize the names of composers such as Sor, Carcassi, Giuliani, Aguado.

Finally, the guitar, as a collection of musical ideas and idiosyncrasies met the first of several geniuses who would significantly further its evolution: Antonio de Torres Jurado. By 1850 he had pulled all the elements together to create the first, and lasting, model of a modern classical guitar. Everything pre-Torres is a guitarlike instrument, belonging in a museum or private collection. A Torres, on the other hand, would not look out of place in the classical room at a local guitar store.

Spanish guitar from Cádiz, 1850, with little decoration except for the rosette

Georg Staufer 6-string guitar, 1820s. Staufer, who taught C. F. Martin, is credited with creating a fretboard that extends to the sound hole.

THE VOBOAM FAMILY built many of the guitars played by the French once they, and their extravagant Sun King, Louis XIV, adopted the instrument in the 17th century. Impeccable craftsmen—at least three members of the family were luthiers, René, Alexandre, and Jean—they were lavish in the use of rare materials, but understood the acoustic importance of keeping decoration away from the working part of the guitar, the top.

*René Voboam 5-course guitar, 1641,
with a fine-grained spruce top*

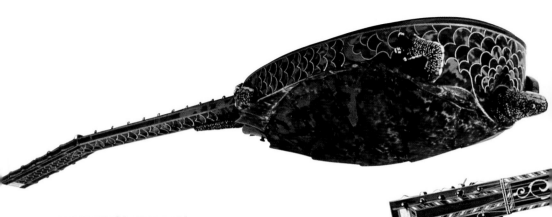

Nicolas Alexandre Voboam II "Tortoise" guitar, 1693. Voboam used the entire carapace; the head, tail, and feet are made of glazed ceramic.

MORE SOUNDS!

Clearly, serious guitarists have been struggling for a long time with the limits of the instrument's design—pushing the boundaries of sound, for example, by adding extra strings to the bass, and compensating for the built-in imperfections of equal temperament created when strings of equal length, but unequal thickness, are stretched over parallel frets.

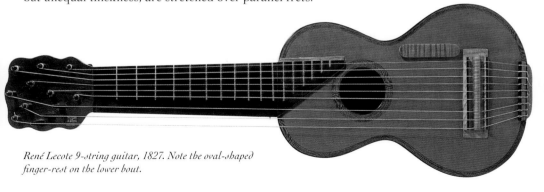

René Lecote 9-string guitar, 1827. Note the oval-shaped finger-rest on the lower bout.

"Enharmonic" guitar, 1829

MORE COMPLICATIONS!

The "enharmonic" guitar was the invention of a Cambridge don trying to create a guitar that could be played in just intonation. Note how the frets are like pegs on a cribbage board, just wide enough for one string and able to move anywhere on the neck. The frets would have to change positions for every key.

ALL THINGS CLASSICAL

In Europe at the end of
the 19th century, in the
midst of a classical revival,
curious hybrids began
appearing in luthiers'
workshops—harp-guitars,
lyre-guitars—that invoked an
idealized Apollonian past
through their marriage
of new and old forms.

Luigi Mozzani
lyre-guitar, 1910

Martin harp-guitar,
c. 1850–60

Emilius Nicolai Scherr harp-guitar,
1830s. Note the harplike long
hollow soundboard that allows the
instrument to stand on the floor.

AN AMERICAN BEAUTY

The American harp-guitar found its true form beginning in the 1890s, when Chris Knutsen, a Norwegian immigrant, designed an instrument with a hollow arm extending out from the body to hold the bass strings. It not only gave the harp-guitar its great look but also contributed to a superior tone. In 1912, his patent for the harp-guitar expired, and by 1917, Chicago's prolifically talented Larson Brothers began making harp-guitars for a Minnesota instrument dealer named W. J. Dyer.

Knutsen harp-guitar, 1912, which also has seven sympathetic strings on the treble side

Dyer Symphony harp-mandolin Style 50, c. 1912–25

Dyer Symphony harp-guitar Style 8, c. 1917–24. Collector Scott Chinery proclaimed this to be the finest-sounding flattop guitar he'd ever played.

Larson harp-guitar, c. 1920, with a plethora of strings and an extra-wide sound hole

JOINED AT THE HIP

Not only did some free-thinking craftsman in the Harmony Company's shop make this Siamese twin of an instrument—but it's known that two or three others exist as well. No one knows what he called it, but a few amusing nicknames have been suggested, including Straddlevarius, Stereosaurus, and Goitar.

SO SIMPLE...

Next to the Torres and other Spanish guitars, this romantic instrument from the 19th century Parisian luthier Etienne La Prevotte seems delicate. One can imagine it barely playing above a whisper.

La Prevotte, mid-19th century, Paris

La Prevotte 11-string, mid-19th century, Paris

AND SO NOT

Requiring a different sort of player altogether is his 11-string guitar. But it has advantages, from the extra bass to greater sustain to most accurate transcriptions from lute music (lutes have 14 or more strings) to expanded possibilities for both player and composer. The most celebrated multistring guitar player was Narciso Ypes, who played a 10-string.

Antonio de Torres Jurado

E very male of a certain age and older understands one of the guitar's primal appeals: its feminine curves. How perfect, then, to learn that according to stories told by his descendents, Antonio de Torres Jurado based his *plantilla* form on the figure of a young woman he saw in Seville. After all, it is Torres's *plantilla* that's given form to virtually every classical guitar made in the subsequent 150 years.

A genius of a luthier, Torres created the modern classical guitar, setting the standards for its size, shape, build, and bracing, and for many of the

lesser details that still predominate. Like a grand chef, he worked with ingredients that basically existed but put them together in a way that made something new, and infinitely better. And in so doing, he changed the idea of what a guitar could do. The instrument came alive with a new range of dynamics and color, of feeling, power, and expressiveness. Its tone was clear, balanced, round, and firm. Ergo Tárrega, ergo Segovia, ergo the guitar as a serious concert instrument.

Born in 1817 in Almería, in southern Spain, Antonio de Torres found local fame in his lifetime but never stopped struggling with poverty and personal adversity. He apprenticed as a carpenter at the age of 12, married not long after that to avoid conscription in the military, endured first the death of two daughters and then his young wife, and finally moved to Seville. A possible detour to Granada in the late 1830s is considered the likely place where he acquired guitar-making skills. However he came by this craft, he was, by the early 1850s, making guitars for flamenco players in a workshop in Seville. By 1856 he produced "La Leona" (the lion),

Antonio de Torres Jurado guitar, 1850s

his first truly great instrument. Two years later, he won a bronze medal in a Seville exhibition with a highly ornamented guitar made out of bird's-eye maple.

Clearly, Torres could build a great-looking guitar if he wanted to (or if the commission came from a wealthy collector). But the true brilliance of Torres's guitars was in how well they played. First, he gave the guitar a larger, deeper body, with a sonically optimum proportion of upper bout to waist to lower bout that was also pleasing to look at (that woman from Seville?) and balanced well on the typical player's body, allowing a greater reach to the upper frets. His string length always

Label inside Torres guitar, from his Second Epoch

hovered around 650mm, the standard today, producing just the right tension: Spaniards call it *tiro de cuerda,* the pull of the string.

Much artistry centered on the top itself. Torres incorporated a seven-strut fan bracing so effective it is still called Torres bracing. He also carved his tops on the thin side for maximum vibration, and "domed" both top and back to make a livelier box with extra strength. In fact, to prove that the top was all-important to the sound, he once, in a famous experiment, created a guitar with papier-mâché back and sides. It performed beautifully. With every element of the guitar—the architectural bridge, the neck angle, mechanical tuners, string spacing, nut width—Torres sought and struck just the right balance.

Torres quit building guitars for a time around 1870 to return to Almería to open a china shop. He resumed again in 1875, coinciding with the end of a civil war in Spain, and thus began his so-called Second Epoch. He continued making his magnificent guitars until 1892, when he died at the age of 75. In all he made 320 instruments, 88 of which are known to still exist. When asked about his secret, he replied: "[It] is one you have witnessed many times, and one that I can't leave to posterity, because it must with my body go to the grave, for it consists of the tactile senses in my finger pads, in my thumb and index finger that tell . . . if the top is or is not well made, and how it should be treated to obtain the best tone from the instrument."

REVOLUTIONARY

Considered the "Stradivari" of luthiers, Torres essentially created the modern classical guitar. One interesting detail to consider, though: Guitars, unlike violins, do not continue to "play" at the height of their powers for centuries. Unlike a violinist picking up a Stradivarius, a guitarist playing a Torres can only imagine how the instrument sounded in its prime.

Antonio de Torres Jurado, 1883, repaired by Manuel Ramirez and Robert Bouchet. It is said to have an unusually long sustain.

Antonio de Torres Jurado, 1888, built toward the end of his career

THE GREAT RAMIREZ

After Torres, the name most associated with developing the Spanish classical guitar is Manuel Ramirez. He was among the first to understand the import of Torres's work and to carry it into the early 20th century. He also famously built the 1912 guitar that a young Segovia used on his climb to international fame. But he didn't just build traditional concert instruments; at one point he had 48 models in his catalog, from the cheapest, unpolished boxes to the sublime Segovia model.

Manuel Ramirez
classical guitar, 1914

GREATS *Andrés Segovia*

For much of the 20th century, Andrés Segovia's name was synonymous with classical guitar. A self-taught master of tone and nuance, of *ribato* and staccato effects, of new techniques and poetic expression, Segovia, in his own words, "rescued the guitar from the hands of flamenco gypsies." Virtually alone he elevated the guitar to its current status as a legitimate concert instrument; for the first time the world heard a guitarist whose virtuosity put him on par with the finest violinist or pianist. The Spanish-born maestro carved a repertoire out of all varieties of early music (including the difficult Bach *Chaconne* for solo violin, stunning audiences) and inspired contemporary composers like Heitor Villa-Lobos and Joaquín Rodrigo to write for him, creating a 20th-century body of classical guitar music. Segovia gave his first concert at the age of 16, in Granada, and his last in April 1987, at the age of 94, dragging his beloved Hauser and Ramirez guitars around the world. He also recorded for 50 years. Finally, he ensured the status of classical guitar by teaching generations of younger players, including Christopher Parkening, Julian Bream, John Williams, and Eliot Fisk.

TEUTONIC ENGINEERING

The first great non-Spanish builder of classical guitars, Germany's Hermann Hauser studied deeply the designs and innovations of Torres, but instead of merely copying the Spaniard's work, he brought to it "his Teutonic engineering principles" (to quote the classical guitarist Julian Bream). The result was guitars of exquisite refinement and yet great tonal power and range. His reputation was secured when Segovia started playing a 1937 Hauser.

Hauser, 1933

Hauser, 1955

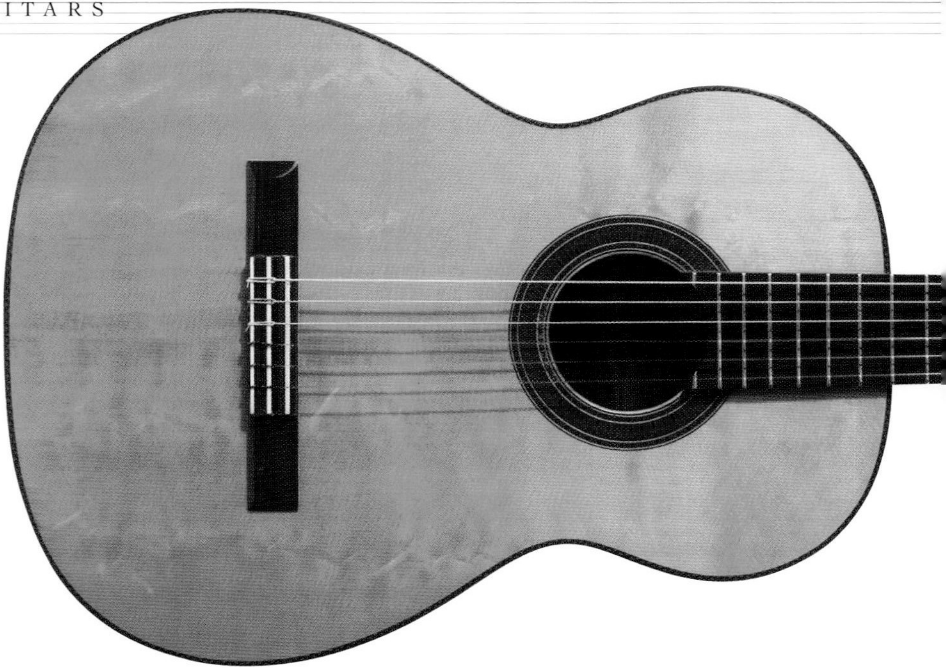

NOT JUST FOR CLASSICAL

A self-taught luthier from
New York, Manouk Papazian
is one of the great underrated
artists. In addition to
attracting classical customers
such as Sharon Isbin and
John Holmquist, his glorious
guitars were also played by
the likes of Paul Stookey
(of Peter, Paul, and Mary)
and the original guitar god,
Duane Eddy.

Manouk Papazian, 1965

Contreras "Carlevaro," 1983

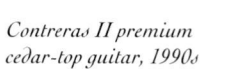

Contreras II premium cedar-top guitar, 1990s

OH CONTRERAS

Manuel Contreras was one of the great Spanish innovators, developing a "double top" guitar in the early 1970s—a second top was suspended beneath the first, to improve tone and volume. Then in 1983 he unveiled the "Carlevaro," inspired by a Uruguayan guitarist. All of its unconventional ideas—lack of a real sound hole, missing waist on the bass side, and extra sides and back to isolate the guitar from the player's body—are intended to increase the instrument's volume and projection. Contreras died in 1994, but his workshop continues.

GUITAR SALON

A well-stocked classical guitar dealer will offer a range from student guitars—many made by famous Spanish workshops—to powerful, and powerfully individual, concert models. Wouldn't it be nice to choose among these?

Edmund Blöchinger, 2004

Enrique Garcia, 1920

Santos Hernandez, 1921

Domingo
Esteso,
1952

Paulino
Bernabé,
2004

Daniel
Friederich,
2006

*Fleta archtop, 1945, one of only
a handful made*

Fleta classical, 1951, with an unusual body of quilted Cuban mahogany

IGNACIO FLETA of Barcelona, Spain, started building classical guitars in 1930 after training as a violin-maker. By the time of his death in 1977, he had a waiting list 15 years long. Idiosyncratic throughout his career, he explored many different ideas, including using untraditional woods, experimenting with steel-string archtops, and changing the strutting pattern and body shape to deliver crisper trebles and greater overall power.

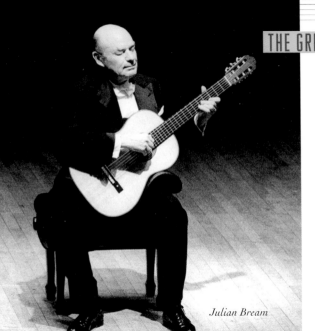

Julian Bream

*Julian Bream
& John Williams*

Largely self-taught, the classical
guitarist Julian Bream began
on the steel-string guitar out of
love for Django Reinhardt's music, and
then heard Segovia playing *Recuerdos de
la Alhambra*. The young Bream brought
his virtuosic technique and emotionally
expressive playing to England in the
'40s, where there was no classical guitar
tradition. Like Segovia, he became a
proselytizer for the instrument, playing
it, writing about it, demystifying it, and

*John
Williams*

encouraging contemporary British composers to create music for it.

André Segovia announced the coming of a very young John Williams with this epithet: "A prince of the guitar has arrived." Williams's gifts were lavish: He could read, play, and master music from virtually any period and any style. Like Bream, he inspired and often commissioned contemporary composers to write for the guitar. But Williams also worked to break down the tight box that defined the classical guitarist. He founded the fusion group Sky, played at Ronnie Scott's jazz club, and even played a duet with The Who's Pete Townshend: "We Won't Get Fooled Again."

THE NEXT MILLENNIUM

Over the last few decades, classical guitarists joined their earlier brethren in a quest for volume. Australian luthier Greg Smallman answered by developing a system of lattice bracing inspired by building and flying model airplanes when he was a boy—the bracing allows for a thinner top while enhancing volume and projection, creating what some describe as an overly percussive sound. Thomas Humphrey built his first Millennium in 1985. This powerful instrument, with the asymmetrical bracing and a negative neck angle that allows greater access to the upper frets, has been called "the only philosophically different classical guitar since Torres."

Greg Smallman's Concert Classical guitar, 1980

Thomas Humphrey's Millennium, 2000, showing negative neck angle

MUY FLAMENCO

Though kissing close, flamenco guitars still differ in key respects from their classical cousins. To achieve its bright, percussive sound, a flamenco guitar is lightly built, to the point of being fragile. It is traditionally made of cypress wood; generally has a shallower body; often uses a light headstock with wooden tuning pegs; and needs the *golpeadores*, the clear tap plates that protect the top from those sharp fingernail blows.

Manuel Reyes, 1983

Marcelo Barbero, 1950, using friction pegs

José Ramirez, 1935. Though most players prefer "blondes," this guitar is a negra, i.e., it has a dark rosewood body.

Archangel Fernandez, 1960

EVOLUTION

Contemporary builder John Monteleone said it this way: "I think that the archtop acoustic is the most romantic and most mysterious of all guitars. The merits of it have long been underestimated and misunderstood . . . there is a good chance that most people seeking an instrument don't even know what a good archtop sounds like, should sound like." Seeking that elusive sound continues to inspire the finest builders.

D'Angelico L-5 style guitar, 1935

Robert Benedetto La Venezia, 2003. Benedetto is a foremost builder of archtop guitars.

John Monteleone's Rocket Convertible, 1995
Two additional sound ports are built into the
side of the guitar and can be opened or closed.
This and other blue archtops were built for the
Scott Chinery Blue Guitar project.

CHAMELEONS

The L-4 was one of Gibson's longest-surviving models, undergoing changes through the decades. Here it is sporting a "snakehead" peghead that its immediate sibling, the L-5, would make legendary.

Gibson L-4 "snakehead," 1924

WHO FIRST?

This Weymann Deluxe from 1925 dazzles with the inlay fretboard and ornate peghead (those are banjo tuners). But the real curiosity is the violin-style f-holes. So whose f-holes came first: those of the world-famous L-5, or this antique from a relatively obscure Philadelphia-based instrument-maker whose name is mostly associated with the banjo?

Weymann Deluxe, 1925, with detail of neck and headstock

400 INCARNATIONS

Based on the old Orville Gibson Style O, the Super 400 made its debut in 1934 and remained Gibson's top-of-the-line jazz guitar—the epitome of the Gibson archtop. Over the years this powerhouse with the full-bodied tone turns up in different incarnations—acoustic, electric, with a cutaway (pointed Florentine or rounded Venetian) and without.

Gibson Super 400, 1937, one of the rare left-handed models

Gibson Super
400CES, 1958. CES
equals "Cutaway
Electric-Spanish,"
a common Gibson
designation.

Gibson Super 400CN,
1959—the "C" for the
Venetian cutaway, the
"N" for its natural finish.

400 KNOCKOFFS

A number of guitar-makers decided to keep Gibson company in the area of 18" acoustic archtops. From the Chicagoans, Regal, a powerful Esquire—light-years from Super 400 standards, but boasting a tasty maple body. Despite the flattop-looking peghead, players had to love the look of stepped tuners. Banjo-maker Bacon also got into the archtop business, producing this 18" Sultana shortly before selling the B&D name to Gretsch in 1940—who then created this Synchromatic 400, with the classy Gretsch styling.

Regal Esquire, 1959

Gretsch Synchromatic 400,
1945

Bacon & Day Sultana,
1930s

*Regal acoustic archtop,
date unknown*

*Hofner President,
1957*

PEOPLE'S INSTRUMENTS

Running counter to the "Super 400" syndrome, any number of makers turned out serviceable archtop guitars for aspiring and performing musicians. The bare-bones Regal with the f-holes that look like they've been designed by stencil belonged to rockabilly star Billy Lee Riley. The more elegant President, made for Selmer UK by the German company Hofner, is exactly the same model that a teenaged George Harrison learned to play on. Vega archtops offered a surprising value, with fine construction and high-quality wood.

Vega Duotron, c. 1948, with floating pickup. Note the controls in the tailpiece and the oversize, translucent tuners.

BOSTON'S FINEST

After several decades of making banjos, drums, and then so-so guitars, Stromberg—father Charles and son, Elmer—came into their heyday in the 1940s and 1950s, building archtop guitars on par with the best Gibsons and D'Angelicos. Strombergs emphasize power. They're braced by a single diagonal running under the top (like half an X-brace) and some, like the top-of-the-line Master 400, reached a massive 19" wide. George Gruhn called them "the loudest guitars in creation." All Strombergs are rare—only 640 were made. The Deluxe Cutaway is among the rarest of the rare.

Stromberg Master 400, 1946

Stromberg Deluxe
Cutaway, 1951

Stromberg G-1,
1945

ONE-UPMANSHIP

Gibson thrives today with its reputation
and history as the finest maker of factory
archtops, but in the 1930s, its New York–
based rival, Epiphone, had an as good, if
not a better, reputation. Thus when Gibson
introduced its 18"-wide Super 400 in 1934,
Epiphone needed to act immediately. The
next year it unveiled the 18½" Emperor,
calling it "handicraft at its finest."
Curiously, the name came out of the year's
big story, when the Duke of Windsor
renounced the throne to marry an American
commoner—Epiphone spun it as the
Emperor and the Maid, and introduced the
new guitar in a photograph showing it posed
with a naked woman (strategically covered
up by the guitar, of course!).

*Epiphone
Emperor,
1949*

Epiphone Triumph
Regent, 1931

Epiphone Emperor
Regent, 1954. "Regent"
means cutaway.

"EXCEL"-LENT

D'Angelicos are among the
most highly valued, highly
sought-after guitars ever
made. Many were custom-
ordered by musicians either
in or traveling through
New York; each has its
own personality. The
Excel, his second-from-
the-top model, was
based on the ongoing
inspiration D'Angelico
found in the Gibson L-5.

D'Angelico Excel,
1942

D'Angelico Excel
Cutaway, 1955

*D'Angelico New Yorker Cutaway
Special—"The Teardrop," 1957*

PRICELESS

One day a local guitarist named Peter Girardi walked into D'Angelico's shop on the Lower East Side and asked him to make him something special to impress his nightclub audiences. D'Angelico came up with an idea to extend the lower body in what he called a "can opener" shape. Years later, after hearing stories about the instrument, the collector Scott Chinery tracked it down, paying $150,000 for it. The next day he was offered $250,000. He not only considered it the best-known and most prestigious vintage guitar anywhere, he was amazed by how it played—turned out that the "teardrop" shape really opened up the sound, creating one of the most powerful archtop guitars Chinery had ever heard.

GREATS *Wes Montgomery*

Wes. At the height of his fame, and among jazz fans ever after, Montgomery achieved the kind of status conferred on an artist known by just one name. He had huge ears and a natural gift, like his hero Charlie Christian, and in fact started playing music professionally by memorizing all of Christian's solos and playing them for local groups. Playing with just the fleshy part of his thumb on a big, hollow-bodied Gibson electric, Wes conveyed extraordinary feeling and power through his rich, round, physical tone, surprising listeners with endlessly inventive musical ideas, including the long single-line solos that dipped into unexpected scale patterns, sophisticated chord melody playing, and the octaves that became his signature sound.

He truly embodied jazz guitar at its best, and has inspired just about every guitarist since. But there is also something cautionary about his tale that may have contributed to the legend of "Wes." Play octaves really well, and then that's all the audience wants to hear. There he was, an all-star, trapped into performing hits for the restless crowds who bought his light pop records.

GROWN-UP GUILDS

Though folkies claim Guild as
the maker of highly regarded
steel-string flattops, the
company had its roots in the
jazz and classical worlds—
jazz, as it arose from the
ashes of Epiphone in the early
1950s, and classical, because
that is what its founder, Al
Dronge, played. The Artist
Award is the one archtop
that withstood the company's
many changes. The hybrid
electric-acoustic A-600B was
made for a trade show but
never went into production.

Guild Artist Award,
1993

Guild A-600B, 1968, with floating DeArmond pickup, oval sound hole, and carved spruce top

UPSCALING

Trying to compete with the big, gutsy archtops from Gibson and D'Angelico, Gretsch introduced the Synchromatic line in the late 1930s, notable for cat's-eye sound holes. Rickenbacker briefly considered doing the same, producing this prototype archtop in 1957. Gretsch also fancied up its flattops with the guitar-pick-shaped sound hole. This model is a cousin of Gretsch's cowboy line of electrics—note the "G" brand on the body and western-themed fingerboard markers.

Gretsch Synchromatic, 1950, with "synchronized" stair-step bridge

Rickenbacker archtop prototype, 1957, with "German curve" around the top

Gretsch Ranger, 1955

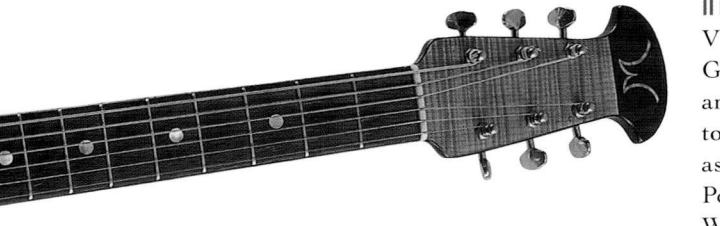

Wilkanowski Airway, c. 1940. Did Ovation designers copy the peghead?

HYBRID?

Violin construction inspired Gibson to create the first archtop guitar, but no luthier took that idea quite as far as Willi Wilkanowski. A Polish-born violin-maker, Wilkanowski opened his own shop in Brooklyn in the late 1930s and turned out some 5,000 violins. But for some mysterious reason he went on a guitar kick between 1938 and 1941, producing about 30 archtop instruments. The plain Airway is his "typical" model.

WORKING IN A BAND

Even after the height of the big-band era and the transition to the solid-body electric guitar, a huge class of guitarists relied on the warm, mellow sound of a hollow-body jazz ax—working-class guitars for refined jazz and pop.

Premiere Deluxe, 1950s

Gibson ES-295, 1954

Gibson L5-CES, 1956, with a Charlie Christian pickup

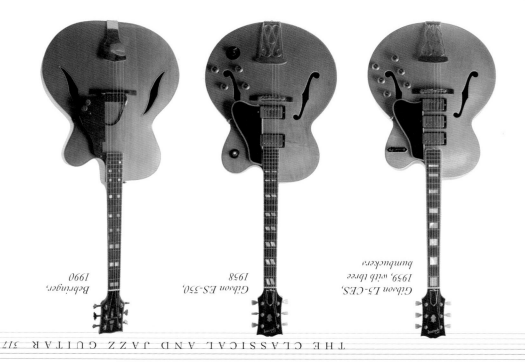

Behringer,
1990

Gibson ES-550,
1958

Gibson L5-CES,
1959, with three
humbuckers

RARE BEAST

Long before Jimmy Page made the Gibson double-neck famous, a player named Art Pruneau ordered this custom L-10. (You can see his name on the six-string peghead.) It is believed to be the only double-neck acoustic archtop Gibson ever made, as well as its first f-hole guitar in a natural finish.

Gibson custom L-10 double-neck, 1936

MARTIN JAZZ

Martin flattops built during
the 1930s are the holy of
holies. But in 1931 the
company also jumped into
the archtop market to reach
players involved in the ever-
more-popular jazz world, and
these models—first built with
round sound holes then more
conventional f-holes—helped
the company survive the
Depression. However, they
were hybrids at best, with their
flat backs, fretboards attached
to—rather than floating
over—the top, and bodies of
rosewood and mahogany.

*Martin F-7, 1938, looking
like the marriage of a Gibson
L-5 and Martin D-45*

Martin F-5, 1940. With its maple body this rare model was the most "archtop"-sounding of the Martin archtops, but it never went into production.

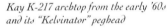

*Kay K-217 archtop from the early '60s
and its "Kelvinator" peghead*

SPECIAL K'S

Kay, one of the big Chicago guitar-makers, sold budget
instruments by the ton. It also offered maple-bodied archtops
for budget-minded players—with a unique peghead variously
described as "Kelvinator" (for the 1950s Sears refrigerator)
and "luncheonette." On the other end of the spectrum is this
Koontz Custom from New Jersey luthier Sam Koontz. Note
how the elaborate scroll cutaway is echoed on the pickguard.

Koontz Custom, 1977

JAZZ GREATS, PLUS TWO

From Nick Lucas on, Gibson sought out artists as
guitar partners, then named the guitars after the
players. These jazz boxes benefit from association
with some of the top players of the day—Barney
Kessel, the great post–Charlie Christian jazz guitarist
who went on to perform both as a celebrated artist
and as a session musician on hundreds of famous pop
recordings; Tal Farlow, bebop guitarist known for his
tremendous speed and rich harmony; Johnny Smith,
one of the most versatile guitarists, whose "Moonlight
in Vermont" is one of the top-selling jazz records of
all time; Howard Roberts, founder of the now-defunct
Guitar Institute of Technology and whose nonjazz
work can be heard on TV themes (*Twilight Zone*,
The Munsters); and two of Nashville's great session
musicians, Billy Byrd and Hank Garland, whose
combined names make Byrdland.

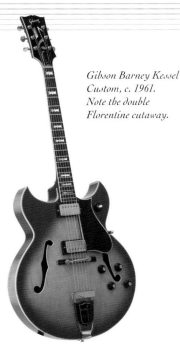

*Gibson Barney Kessel
Custom, c. 1961.
Note the double
Florentine cutaway.*

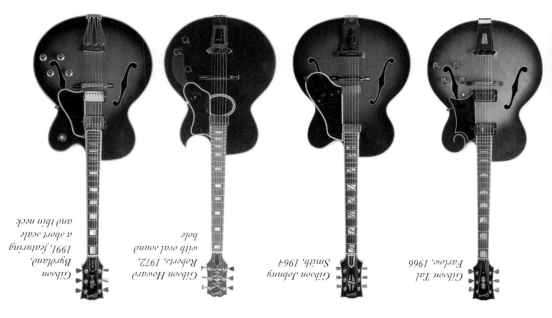

Gibson
Byrdland,
1991, featuring
a short scale
and thin neck

Gibson Howard
Roberts, 1972,
with oval sound
hole

Gibson Johnny
Smith, 1964

Gibson Tal
Farlow, 1966

APPRENTICE TO MASTER

One day a fledgling guitarist named Jimmy D'Aquisto walked into John D'Angelico's Manhattan workshop, and never wanted to leave. Little by little D'Angelico tolerated this apprentice, giving him this basic instruction: "This is what I want done and this is how I do it. You do it any way you like, but it must turn out as good or better than what I did." And it did. After D'Angelico's death, D'Aquisto became the country's premier archtop builder, setting up shop in Long Island and producing some 370 instruments.

D'Aquisto solo noncutaway, 1992–93. In models like this, D'Aquisto literally changed the course of archtop design—and clearly worked away from D'Angelico's ideas about decoration.

D'Aquisto Solo Special,
1995, a one-of-a-kind
instrument inspired
by D'Angelico's unique
"Teardrop" New Yorker

D'Aquisto "Advance,"
1994. Note the sliding
sound hole covers.

TAKE YOUR PICK

After nearly disappearing in the postwar years as
a viable instrument, the acoustic archtop is making
a comeback through the hands of skilled luthiers
who are attracted to the form's challenges and
possibilities. Canadian builder Michael Greenfield
offers several standard models, including the
small-bodied 15" Newport, which has a jazz "pop"
along with the balance needed for intimate, fingerstyle playing, and his traditional 17" Vanguard,
a complete package of tone (full, round, open),
playability, power—and, obviously, looks.

Greenfield Newport,
2004

*Greenfield Vanguard,
2006. Both are carved
from cello woods.*

FIVE

Plugged In!

Burns Bison, 1961

THE PEOPLE'S INSTRUMENT

How lucky it must have felt to be a kid in the early 1960s, before the decade grew too dark and strange, and to wake up on Christmas morning to find a large rectangular box under the tree. You open it, breathless with excitement, and it's just what you'd hoped: a black case that not only held your first electric guitar, a Silvertone, but had the amp built into it, too. Talk about plug and play! The whole outfit cost about $70 and was sold exclusively through Sears. Wonder how many of those guitars were cranking out "A Hard Day's Night" after a few lessons?

There's an infamous line spoken by the he-shall-remain-nameless Decca A&R man who passed on signing The Beatles in 1962: "We don't like their sound. Groups of guitars are on their way out." Ouch! Well, hindsight, as the cliché goes, is 20/20, and taste is a personal thing. But even by 1962 it should have been clear that the guitar had taken over the world of popular music.

Guitars were everywhere, and in a profusion of styles. There was Elvis, gyrating to a D-18 that he'd covered in tooled leather. Buddy Holly playing a sunburst Stratocaster. Chuck Berry duckwalking with his ES-355. Muddy Waters

and his red Tele. Les Paul with his Les Paul. The early Beatles with their matching Rickenbackers. Bo Diddley and the "Big B," the one-of-a-kind rectangular ax built for him by Gretsch. Brian Jones and his teardrop Vox. Wes Montgomery and his mellow Gibson L5-CES. There were the black roots guitarists rediscovered during the folk revival—Leadbelly and his 12-string Harmony, Bukka White playing slide on a National, southpaw Elizabeth Cotton fingerpicking "Freight Train" on her reverse-strung Martin 00-18. For a while, even classical guitars became hot, through British musicians like Julian Bream and John Williams, the pop filigree of Chet Atkins, and the nylon string bossa nova of Antonio Carlos Jobim, who teamed up with Frank Sinatra for a very hot "cool" record.

National/Supra Airline, made for Montgomery Ward, late 1950s. The case contains the amplifier.

And, of course, there was Jimi Hendrix, who more than any other player pushed the limits of the guitar, including, famously, setting one on fire in a ritualistic display at the Monterey Pop Festival.

This wave lifted all boats: acoustics and electrics, cheap guitars and fancy guitars. But it was the solid-body electric—truly, the people's guitar—that epitomized the instrument's cultural surge in popularity.

Wurlitzer Wildcat, 1960s

The fact is, when Les Paul built his Frankenstein-like "The Log" and when Leo Fender went to the drawing board to design a mass-producible Telecaster, it was an act of liberation. No longer was a guitar bound by the physics of strings over a resonating chamber. Now it was almost more of a collection of ideas than an instrument. Everything changed: the tone, the body, the size, the shape, the volume, and that amazing solid-body sustain. Talk about sustain! (After Gibson built its prototype Les Paul, it realized it had to do something to the solid maple body: The thing never shut up. It solved this problem by dampening the body with a mahogany cap.)

Purists questioned whether a solid-body electric was even a guitar at all; wasn't it just some hyped-up machine for making noise? Or take our imaginary purist one step further: Was Jimi Hendrix playing a guitar, or had he mastered a mazelike connection of signals and electronics, composing on the spot with effects and distortion, using the guitar less like an instrument and more like an interface? It almost sounds convincing until a young guitarist tries to learn "Little Wing." Hendrix could *play* as brilliant with his Strat as Segovia was with his Hauser.

All of which is irrelevant for the kids. Plug it in, crank it up, and be happy. The only "music" you needed to know were three chords and a few single-

Gibson Firebird, 1964

note solos, which in a way harkened all the way back to the 17th and 18th centuries, when the guitar had a reputation as a peasant's instrument, not worthy of serious study. Electric guitars were loud, rude, inexpensive, not always so reliable (particularly when it came to their partner, the amplifier), gaudy, colorful, and either exhilarating or threatening, depending on how old you were.

Gretsch Monkees model, 1967

More than anything, those first electric guitars were fun, pure and simple. When Chuck Berry laid down the basic architecture for rock 'n' roll in his song "Maybellene"—i.e., teens, love, and cars—to a backbeat, he released a spirit as liberated as the guitar itself.

And electric guitars were also desirable. They were objects—of lust, of transformation. (Buy one! Be a star!) They were part and parcel of the speeded-up postwar years of television, the space race, better living through chemistry, the Top 40, and the youth revolution, and everything nascent marketers were discovering about a new generation's buying power. When, for example, George Harrison appeared on the Ed Sullivan show playing his Gretsch Country Gentleman, the company had to ramp up production to 100 electrics a day, seven days a week, and still fell a year behind in back orders. From 1955 until the mid-'70s, Fender manufactured a quarter of a million Telecasters. That's a lot of twang!

One good analogy is to the American automobile. Once upon a time, all cars were Ford Model Ts in basic black. Then General Motors appeared, and soon all hell broke loose. Well, once upon a time, guitars were all white or blond Telecasters, then Gibson showed up, and then. . . . Out of the blue, it seemed, new makers appeared, companies like Peavey, Ampeg, Alembic, Mosrite, BC Rich, Veleno. The colors were delicious, Gretsch's and Fender's in particular: Lake Placid Blue Metallic, Jaguar Tan, Surf Green, Bordeaux Burgundy, Fiesta Red, silvers and golds, sparkles and paisleys. The gadgets were multiplying. The Telecaster started with two knobs and a selector switch; the Strat added another pickup, requiring another knob. There were guitars that came with built-in stands, built-in amps, built-in light shows, and by the end of the '60s, full-on onboard electronics, with enough buttons and switches to make an airline pilot feel at home. And what names: Mustang. Jaguar. White Falcon. Marauder. The Futura. The Flying V. Palomino. Malibu. Duo-Jet, Astro-Jet, and Silver Jet. Firebird and Thunderbird. Corvette. The Bikini. Polara. Orbiter. National in particular specialized in upscale, vaguely California-ish sounding names: Bel-Aire, Glenwood, Belmont, Westwood, Newport 82, Town and Country.

And today, of course, there's even *more* variety, *more* possibilities, *more* changes. Gibson unveiled the first all-digital guitar. Daisy Rock produces a full line of girl's guitars. There are so many variations on a Strat that you could buy a new one every month.

So what is being plugged in? A guitar? A tool for self-expression? A statement? A lifestyle? A dream?

All of the above.

Daisy Rock Atomic Pink, 2007

Fender Stratocaster,
"Brownie," 1956
(front and back)

Cigarette burn on
the headstock

BROWNIE

Few guitars are known by name—this is one of the most famous, the 1956 sunburst Stratocaster belonging to Eric Clapton and played on perhaps his most famous track, "Layla." Clapton was inspired to pick up a Strat after seeing one of his heroes, Buddy Guy, playing his at London's Marquee Club. It cost him £150 (about $200) in 1967; it was auctioned off at Christie's in 1999 for $450,000.

EYE CANDY

Gibson made the first strong
statement about electric
guitars' looks when it released
its Les Paul as a bright gold-
top. Ever since, guitar-makers
high and low have used color as
a powerful allure for the player.
Here's a rainbow across the
color spectrum.

*Harmony
Stratotone
Newport, 1957*

*Thomas Custom,
c. 1962*

Ibanez Jem,
1980s

Kay Double Cutaway
K 592, c. 1964

Soulfool in the
Telecaster style,
2006

*Rickenbacker 331,
c. 1971, in all its glory*

Fender Telecaster, 1968

FAR OUT

There's something bizarre about a Telecaster, the most blue-collar of guitars, decked out in pink paisley. It was one of two Flower Power Teles Fender released in 1968. Rickenbacker's 331 light show seems perfect for the summer of love and hallucinogens, but in fact the short-lived model didn't appear until 1971; its most famous venue was the country corn variety program *Hee Haw*, where Buck Owens liked to show it off.

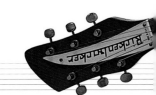

THE FUTURE, WHAT A CONCEPT

Gibson needed guitars to compete with the "future has arrived" Stratocaster. The bizarre Moderne appeared in drawings in 1958, but was put on hold for a few more decades. Gibson's recent reissue of the Futura, originally a sibling of its far more successful Flying V, sports a V-shaped head. Years later, Ken Parker would also try to usher in the future of electric guitars with his Fly. It combines a mix of magnetic and piezo pickups and has a lightweight, resonant wood body strengthened with composite materials.

Gibson Moderne, which finally appeared in 1982

Gibson custom Futura, 2002

"It looks like something you found on the beach."

—JONI MITCHELL, COMMENTING ON
THE FLY TO ITS CREATOR, KEN PARKER

*Parker Fly Artist, 2000—
one of the lightest and most
versatile electric guitars made*

PARALLEL STREAM

In a world dominated by two
names, Fender and Gibson,
smaller builders like Guild still
managed decades of growth,
innovation, and influence.
First known for its big jazz
archtops, Guild tried it all.
The company built the fabulous
solid-body Thunderbird S-200,
with its built-in stand—this one
belonged to Muddy Waters;
the thinline Starfires—Mike
Mitchell of The Kingsmen
banged out "Louie Louie" on
this Starfire II; and the semi-
hollow Aristocrat M-75—this one
belonged to John Lee Hooker.

*Guild Thunderbird
S-200, 1966. Note
the stand on the back.*

Guild Aristocrat M-75, 1959

Guild Starfire II, 1966

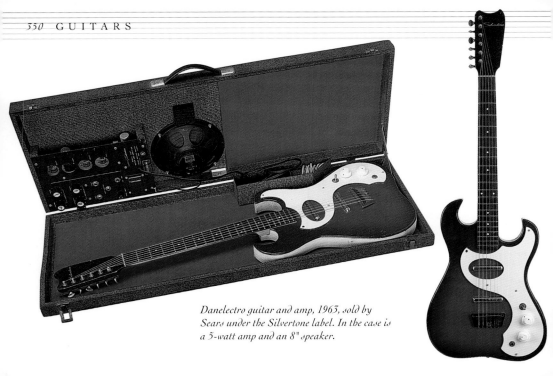

*Danelectro guitar and amp, 1963, sold by
Sears under the Silvertone label. In the case is
a 5-watt amp and an 8" speaker.*

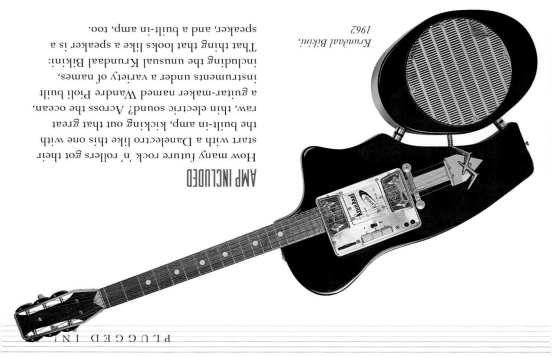

AMP INCLUDED

How many future rock 'n' rollers got their start with a Danelectro like this one with the built-in amp, kicking out that great raw, thin electric sound? Across the ocean, a guitar-maker named Wandre Pioli built instruments under a variety of names, including the unusual Krundaal Bikini: That thing that looks like a speaker is a speaker, and a built-in amp, too.

Krundaal Bikini,
1962

HEADLESS

For all its flash, the solid-body electric is fairly conservative in design principles: body, one or two cutaways, long neck, trademark headstock. And then there are these avant-garde, aerodynamic, unguitarlike guitars. You can almost imagine your fretting hand flying off the neck.

*Modulus Graphite
Flight 6 Monologue,
1983*

*Steinberger,
1986*

Klein BF, 1998, a mash-up of styles from the retro "lipstick tube" neck and center pickup to the high-tech locking tremelo

GREATS *Jimi Hendrix*

It is hard to remember that the guitar god of all guitar gods enjoyed a paltry four years of fame before dying at the age of 27. And it only adds to the sense of otherworldliness of his life. He chased sounds that no one else heard, tied his soaring, sonic flights to the earthiness of blues and rock and roll. But to get there he had to travel a well-worn slog on the chitlin circuit, playing with Little Richard, The Isley Brothers, King Curtis, Ike and Tina Turner, Sam Cooke, Wilson Pickett. By 1965 he was in New York with his own band, Jimmy James and the Blue Flames, when Animals bassist Chas Chandler "discovered" him at the Café Wha? and persuaded Hendrix to move to London. There, forming The Experience with Noel Redding and Mitch Mitchell, Hendrix dazzled British rock royalty like Eric Clapton and Pete Townshend. In the summer of 1967, Hendrix set his guitar—and the music world—on fire at the Monterey Pop Festival; by the time he got to Woodstock, he headlined as the top act (earning $18,000) and performed his unforgettable version of "The Star-Spangled Banner." A year later he was gone, but he left behind hundreds of hours of music recorded at his own studio, Electric Ladyland.

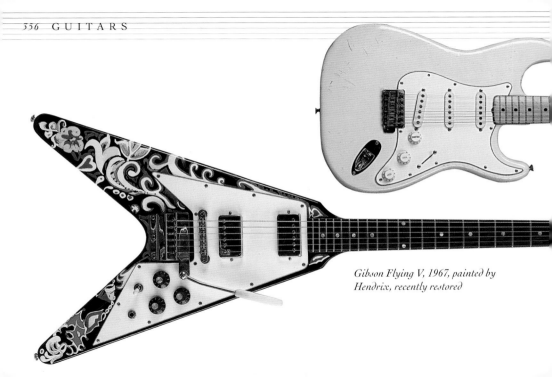

Gibson Flying V, 1967, painted by Hendrix, recently restored

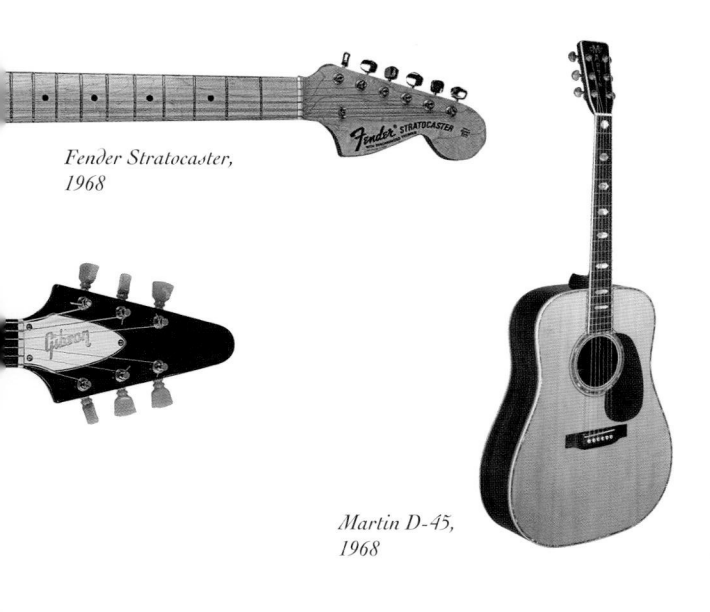

Fender Stratocaster, 1968

Martin D-45, 1968

THE HENDRIX ARSENAL

No other player before or since Jimi Hendrix used the electric guitar to such expressive effect. He most often played Stratocasters, right-handed models that were reverse-strung, but he also owned three Gibson Flying Vs, including this 1967 model that he himself painted. (The guitar was fully restored in 1999; the paintwork is an authentic reproduction of the original.) The real surprise for many fans is to hear the rare recording of him playing an acoustic. That's Hendrix's Martin D-45.

*Ruokangas Defense of Sampo, 2000,
which features inlay work illustrating
a chapter from the Finnish national
epic, the* Kalevala

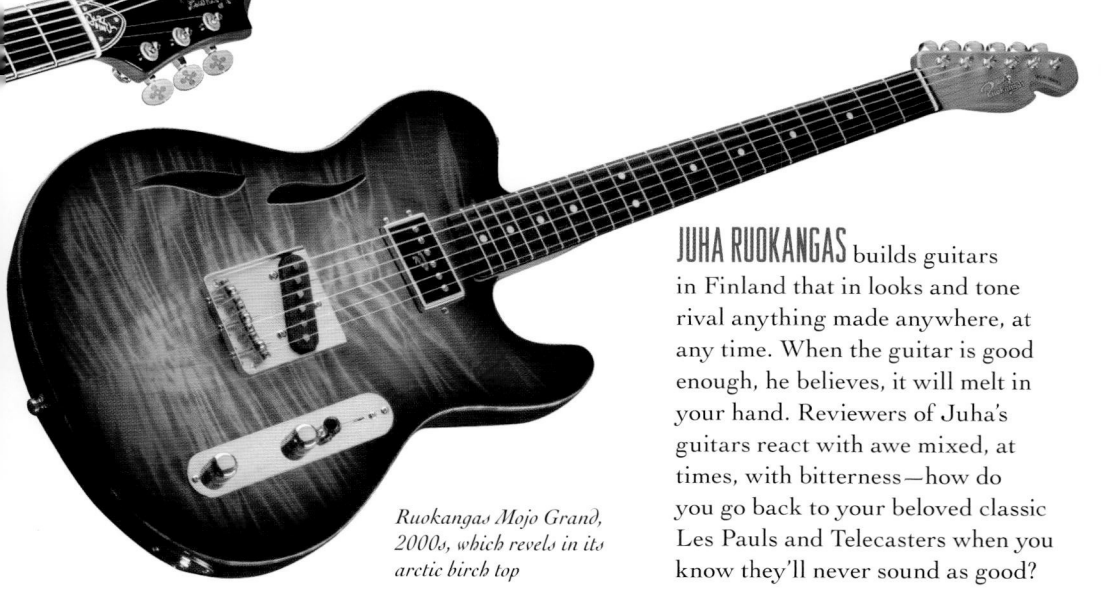

JUHA RUOKANGAS builds guitars in Finland that in looks and tone rival anything made anywhere, at any time. When the guitar is good enough, he believes, it will melt in your hand. Reviewers of Juha's guitars react with awe mixed, at times, with bitterness—how do you go back to your beloved classic Les Pauls and Telecasters when you know they'll never sound as good?

Ruokangas Mojo Grand, 2000s, which revels in its arctic birch top

HOT RODS

By the 1940s, former partners of the National Dobro Company—yep, them again—founded Valco and started manufacturing some of the coolest electric guitars ever. The 1960s models made out of Res-O-Glas are especially stylish. And hotter than ever, now that Jack White of the White Stripes uses them for his down-and-dirty guitar work.

National Airline, 1962

National Glenwood, 1955

*National
Glenwood 95,
1965*

*National
Glenwood 99,
c. 1965*

*Supro
Belmont,
1962*

THE ICON, CONTINUED

Legend has it that Les Paul himself picked the gold color of the original Les Paul because it looked "expensive." The same legend has him picking the black on the solid mahogany Les Paul Custom, nicknamed "Black Beauty" and "Fretless Wonder."

Gibson Les Paul, 1952, a classic first-year "Gold-Top," with the P-90 soapbar pickups and trapeze tailpiece that caused intonation problems

Gibson Les Paul "Black Beauty," 1955, belonging to Jimi Hendrix and outfitted with a Bigsby

Gibson Les Paul Custom Deluxe, 1963

Gibson Les Paul Anniversary Model, 1979

LES WHO?

Paul's name is on the Custom Deluxe, but by 1963 it was probably already called an "SG" (for "Solid Guitar"). Twenty-five years after the beginning, the Anniversary Model.

TV SPECIALS

It's the great confluence of postwar cultural trends: electric guitars on TV! Sensing the opportunity in broadcasting to a wide audience—and just adding a little sexiness to what is essentially a plain-Jane model—Gibson introduced the Les Paul TV Special in 1955. Its distinguishing characteristic is the mustard-yellow color that, the thinking went, would show up nicely on black-and-white television while getting around the glare problem of the all-white.

Gibson Les Paul TV Special, 1957

Gibson Les Paul Junior TV,
1961, with the SG shape that
Paul disowned

Gibson Les Paul Junior TV,
1959, with single pickup

THE HIGHEST FORM OF FLATTERY?

An entire book could be filled with Les Paul knockoffs. Here are just two, from near and far. By the way, Gibson started suing its more threatening imitators in 1977, first Ibanez and later PRS.

Hagstrom Swede, 1970s, from Sweden

Ross Teigen "Les Poulet," 1992. The pointy-bottomed Teigen marries the sensibilities of Florida-based luthier Ross Teigen with classic Les Paul colors and appointments.

Gibson ES-335, 1963

HEY, PAUL

Classical musicians naturally move up the ladder from student models to the very finest concert instruments they can afford—or adopt, on loan from a benefactor. Not so in the pop world. On the far left, an impeccable dot-neck sunburst Gibson ES-335, a guitar from a magnificent vintage. Next to it is the guitar Paul McCartney played, literally—his Epiphone Casino, the cheap version of a Gibson. It just had that "sound." (John and George used them too.)

Paul McCartney's Epiphone Casino, 1962

*Mosrite Custom
guitar, 1980*

SEMIE MOSELEY

got his start working for Rickenbacker before heading out on his own, first building crazy custom guitars in the 1950s and peaking in 1968 when his company, Mosrite, made 600 guitars a month, a number made possible by the endorsement of Nokie Edwards of The Ventures. Still, there was always time for Moseley the luthier to create extraordinary custom work, like the Strawberry Alarm Clock guitars (page 405) and the stunning instrument he made in 1980 for a business partner.

Mosrite Joe Maphis, 1960s

Mosrite Ventures, 1960s

NECK PLUS

In 1984, the future looked like this: From Japan came the Roland G-707 guitar-synthesizer. Hard to know if the second-neck-like stabilizer bar intrigued or alienated players, but it did not find many takers.

Roland G-707, 1984

Bigsby Double-neck, 1952. Grady Martin played this custom instrument on hundreds of recordings in Nashville.

PRE-STRAT

The future arrived a bit prematurely when Paul Bigsby built the very first electric instrument of its kind, a double-neck guitar/mandolin for session player Grady Martin. The guitar part had an unheard-of three pickups. A few years later, Fender would launch its own three-pickup guitar called the Stratocaster with a very similar peghead. By the way, the Bigsby name turns up often in the early history of electric guitars—he invented the Bigsby vibrato arm and tailpiece, prominent on this instrument.

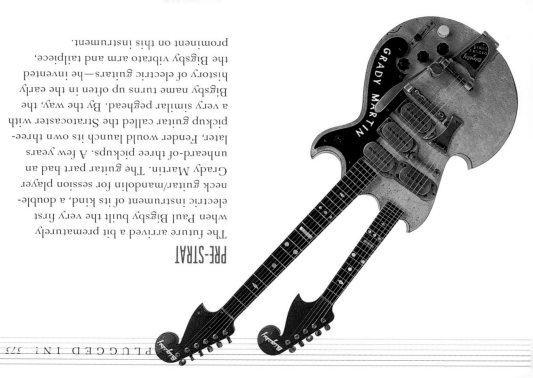

LOOK, MA! TEN HANDS!

Conventional double-necks put a 6-string and 12-string guitar in a player's hands at the same time. Interesting that the first to produce it, circa 1954, came from left field—or Springfield, Missouri, through a blip of a company called Stratosphere.

Stratosphere double-neck, c. 1954

Billy Roberts custom double-neck, 1970s

*Hamer custom
5-neck, 1981, built
for Rick Nielsen of
Cheap Trick. Nielsen
really played this
during his years on
the road—wonder
which tech kept its
36 strings in tune.*

*Danelectro Coral
Sitar, 1968*

ELECTRIC ECCENTRIC

The solid-body guitar concept and the newfound rock 'n' roll market liberated instrument builders' imaginations. Danelectro, inspired by studio guitarist Vinnie Bell, merged east and west with its Coral Sitar—with drone strings and a "buzz" bridge—and its electric Bellzouki, one of the first electric 12-string guitars (its name suggested by its resemblance to a Greek bouzouki). Vox brought out a pint-sized 12-string called the Mando-Guitar for its mandolin-like shape and tone.

*Vox Mando-Guitar,
1960s*

*Danelectro Bellzouki, early
1960s*

12-STRINGS

It's the chimey, Beatle-y, indelible sound of mid-1960s happy rock and roll. And no wonder: Electric 12-strings were just nibbling around an untapped market when Rickenbacker devised the 360/12 and sent one to George Harrison in 1964. Then Roger McGuinn bought one after watching *A Hard Day's Night,* and the electric 12-string enjoyed its first big burst of popularity in what would become an ebb-and-flow history.

Rickenbacker 450/12, 1966

Fender 12-string, 1968

Gibson ES-335 12-string, 1966

Vox Phantom XII Stereo, c. 1965

MULTIPLE PERSONALITIES

Though Fender didn't
invent the idea of hot,
custom colors for a guitar,
they took it farther than
anyone else. Are they
Strats or bowling balls?

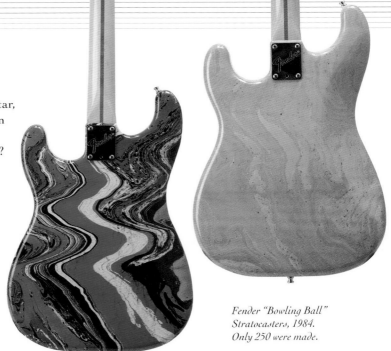

*Fender "Bowling Ball"
Stratocasters, 1984.
Only 250 were made.*

WHERE AM I?

Gibson, on the other hand, seemed drawn to experiment with shapes. It's a guitar! It's a map! Introduced first as an Epiphone, then with the Gibson label, the map guitar went into limited production in the early '80s. It even plays well, though owners should be careful with Maine and Florida.

Gibson Map Guitar,
1982–83

SOMETIMES IT'S ALL ABOUT THE WOOD ...

With a 2" nut—for players with hands like a lumberjack?—
and exotic woods used everywhere (the knobs, the
pickguard), everything about this Abe Rivera "purple
burst" Sceptre feels substantial. (It's usually an Abe
Rivera in Kevin Eubanks's hands on *The Tonight Show*.)
The Alembic Jerry Garcia is a tribute both to the artist
and to the guitars that Doug Irwin built for Garcia,
with its combination of amazing electronics
and sandwich of woods, including
Cocobolo, maple, and vermillion. The
German maker Hoyer had a field day
carving the wood on this striking
Bianca.

Abe Rivera
Sceptre, c. 2000

Hoyer Bianka, 1961

Alembic Jerry Garcia, 2006

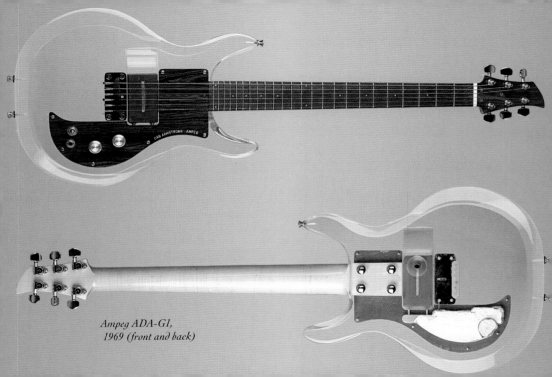

Ampeg ADA-G1,
1969 (front and back)

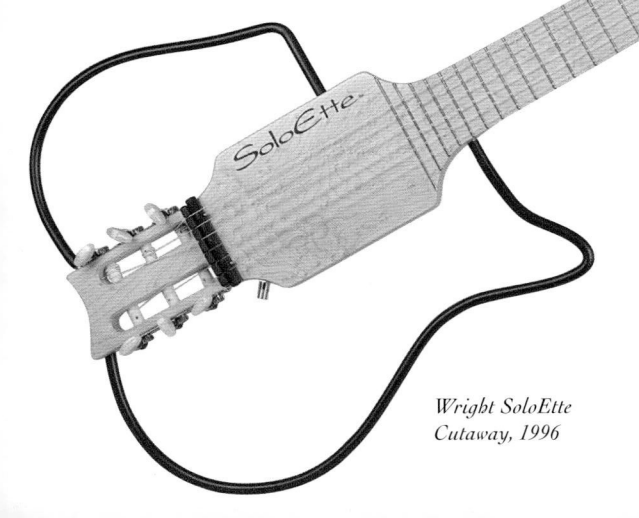

*Wright SoloEtte
Cutaway, 1996*

... AND SOMETIMES IT'S NOT

Remember when everything came in Lucite? Ampeg, known for its excellent amplifiers, hired Dan Armstrong, a guitar repairman in New York, to create the short-lived See-Through line of guitars. This model has three interchangeable pickups for different styles, from growl to pure. From a company called Wright Guitar Technology in Eugene, Oregon, comes the SoloEtte, a bodiless travel guitar.

Zemaitis, 1970s, looking like a Les Paul impersonating a cowboy belt buckle

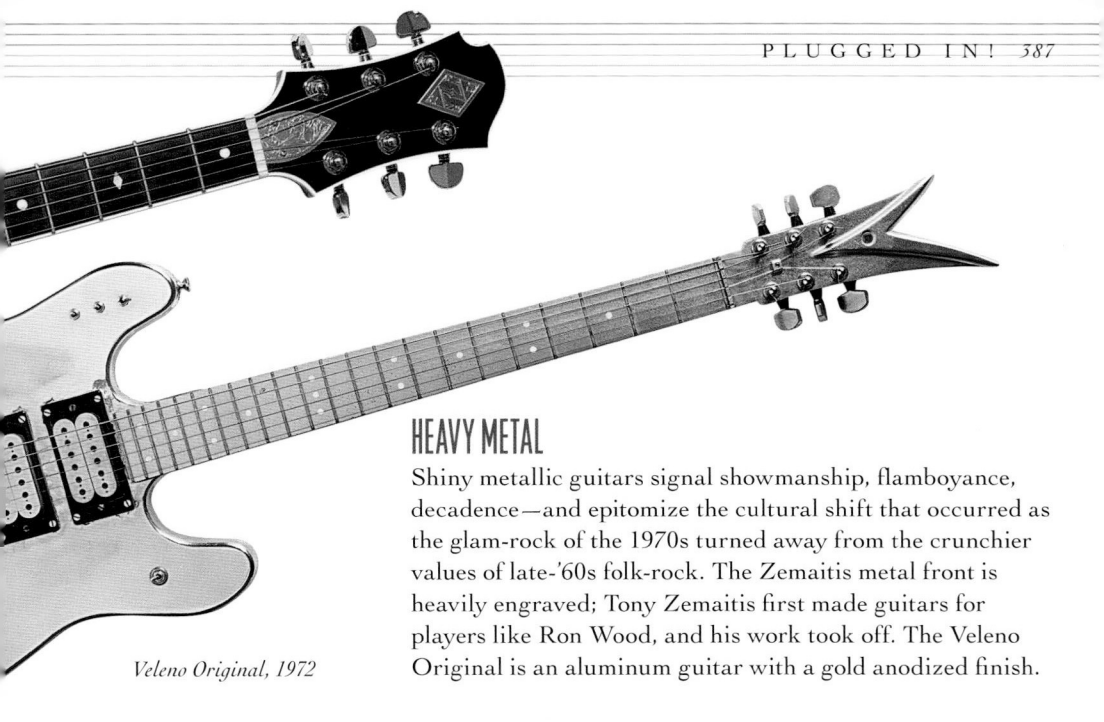

HEAVY METAL

Shiny metallic guitars signal showmanship, flamboyance, decadence—and epitomize the cultural shift that occurred as the glam-rock of the 1970s turned away from the crunchier values of late-'60s folk-rock. The Zemaitis metal front is heavily engraved; Tony Zemaitis first made guitars for players like Ron Wood, and his work took off. The Veleno Original is an aluminum guitar with a gold anodized finish.

Veleno Original, 1972

BRITISH INVASION

The Vox sound—clean, clear, often called "chimey"—pretty much defined the British Invasion from The Beatles (who used Vox amps) onward. Vox also made guitars, developing the famous teardrop for doomed Rolling Stones guitarist Brian Jones. The rarer Vox Bulldog was actually made for Vox in Italy—the Italian invasion—and astute readers will see that it's really a Mosrite Ventures copy.

Vox "Tear Drop," 1965

Vox Bulldog, 1960s

BURNS is a legendary British company whose highly playable guitars cover the design spectrum.

1961
Burns Bison,

Burns Marvin, 1964.
The scroll headstock was
codesigned with Hank
Marvin of The Shadows.

GREATS *Chuck Berry*

By some measures, Chuck Berry is easily the most influential guitarist ever, inspiring the music, the players, and the fans that would make the guitar the central instrument of the 20th century. As John Lennon said, "If you tried to give rock and roll another name, you might call it Chuck Berry." Through his Gibson guitar and songwriting gifts, Berry gave hillbilly swing a driving beat, infused 12-bar blues with the fresh subjects of cars, kids, and young love, and served up a twangy, bluesy, boogie-woogie guitar style filled with riffs, percussive rhythm, and stabbing double-stops. He put the guitar right out in front, as in the famous, joyous opening of "Johnny B. Goode." Everybody copied him. His songs from the mid-1950s, such as "Maybellene," "Rock and Roll Music," "Roll Over Beethoven," "School Days," and "Sweet Little Sixteen," essentially created rock and roll guitar music, making him the godfather of every kid who wanted to plug in. (On inducting him into the Rock and Roll Hall of Fame, Keith Richards confessed, "It's hard for me to induct Chuck Berry, because I lifted every lick he ever played!") Perhaps all too tellingly, his only song ever to reach number one was the winking novelty number, "My Ding-a-Ling."

*Gibson B.B. King Super
Lucille, 2000s*

Gibson ES-355, 1973, signed by Chuck Berry

KILLER GIBSONS

Behold Chuck Berry's ax—or at least one of them—with its stereo controls, missing tone bar, signature, and doodle. He owned this instrument in the early 1970s, and it's easy to imagine it being duckwalked across a flashy stage. There were many "Lucilles" in B.B. King's life before Gibson took his red 1968 ES355-TDSV and transformed it, in 1982, into the official artist model.

PICKUP LINES

A guitar pickup is a transducer—a type of electronic or electromagnetic device that converts physical energy into electrical energy. In this case, it converts the string's vibrations into electrical pulses that are then amplified and turned back into sound waves by a loudspeaker. Here are the basic models.

"Charlie Christian Pickup"—an early bar pickup that produces a clear, powerful jazz tone, named after guitarist Charlie Christian.

Fender Single-Coil—Leo Fender used six magnetic pole pieces, one for each string, with a "single coil" of wire running around them, resulting in a bright, punchy sound that can veer to "ice-pick" on the treble end.

Gibson P-90—Gibson's beefier version of the single-coil, with a rich but still bright sound that falls midway between classic Fender and classic humbucker.

Humbucker—single-coil pickups hum—they're like antennas, picking up disturbances and converting them into a 60-cycle hum, a.k.a. noise. In 1954, Seth Lover invented the dual-coil, noise-canceling—"buck the hum"—pickup, resulting in the darker, fatter, bluesier sound of a Gibson Les Paul.

Piezo Pickup—piezoelectric transducers use crystals or ceramic to register small changes in pressure produced by the strings. They're mounted directly under the bridge and are used most often for acoustic guitars, where, for example, they can pick up the vibrations of a nylon string, which magnetic pickups cannot. Piezos deliver a relatively pure acoustic tone and are particularly good at registering upper-frequency sounds.

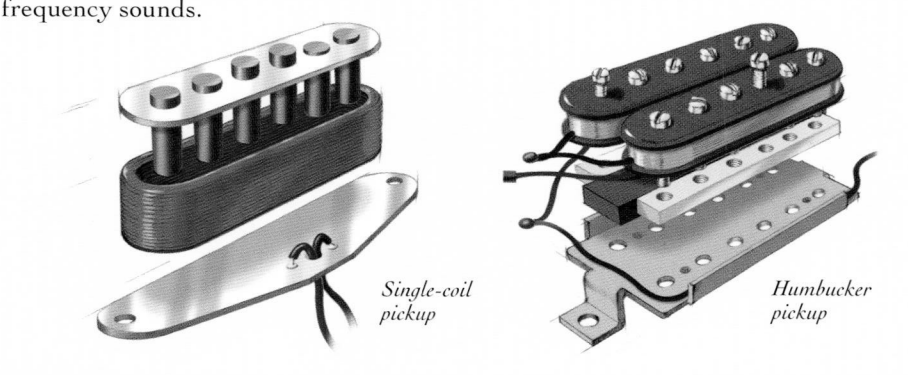

Single-coil pickup

Humbucker pickup

DO YOU WANT ONE PICKUP WITH THAT?

There's something to be said for simplicity. Down and dirty, these single pickup models were great entry-level guitars for young rockers in the '60s.

Danelectro, 1953

Harmony Stratotone, 1953, once owned by Carl Perkins

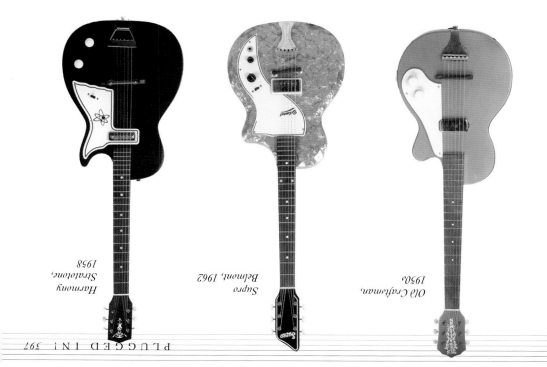

Harmony
Stratotone,
1958

Supro
Belmont, 1962

Old Craftsman,
1950s

...OR TWO?

More tone, more choices, and the occasional whammy bar. Plus, in the case of the very rare 1965 Framus Strato-Melody from Germany, a particularly unusual configuration of nine strings: three single strings on the bass and three doubled-up strings on the treble, just like a 12-string.

Kent, 1965, owned by Delta bluesman Sam Carr

Mysterious semihollow electric, 1960s

Framus Strato-Melody 1965

Kay Solo King, c. 1958

Guitar belonging to western swing-musician Spade Cooley, 1950s

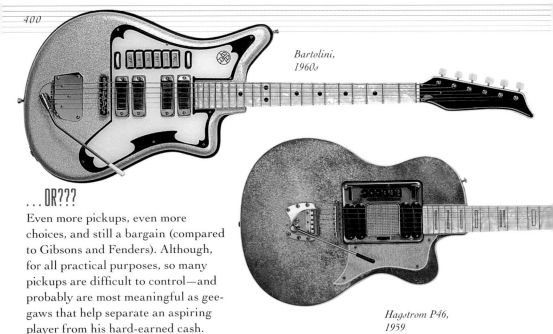

Bartolini,
1960s

...OR???

Even more pickups, even more
choices, and still a bargain (compared
to Gibsons and Fenders). Although,
for all practical purposes, so many
pickups are difficult to control—and
probably are most meaningful as gee-
gaws that help separate an aspiring
player from his hard-earned cash.

Hagstrom P46,
1959

Eko 700/4V,
1964

Selova, 1960s,
with 6 pickups, one
for each string

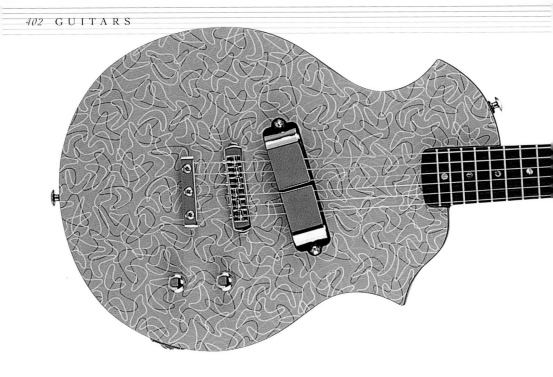

PLAYING HORSESHOES

It's a blues and bottleneck player's dream machine, the Rick Turner Model T with a double-horseshoe pickup reminiscent of the original Rickenbacker Frying Pan.

Rick Turner Model T,
1999

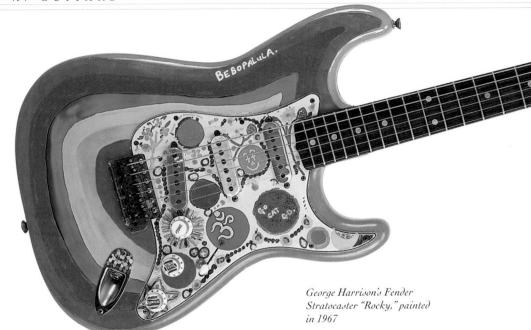

George Harrison's Fender Stratocaster "Rocky," painted in 1967

MAGICAL MYSTERIES

George Harrison hand-painted his Strat, labeled it "Rocky," and played it on *The Magical Mystery Tour* and thereafter. Outlasting Strawberry Alarm Clock's one great hit, "Incense and Peppermints," are the 6-string and 12-string custom instruments made for the band by Semie Moseley. Von Dutch, the legendary painter and pinstriper of '50s and '60s motorcycles and hot rods, did the paint job.

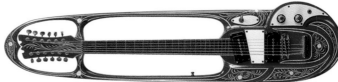
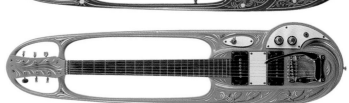

Semie Moseley custom-made 6-string and 12-string guitars, 1967

Leo Fender

How "only in America" to learn that the man whose innovations changed modern music couldn't read a note. Or that the masterful inventor who gave the world the Telecaster, Stratocaster, and Precision Bass not only couldn't play the guitar, rumor says he couldn't even tune it.

Leo Fender, a farmboy from Anaheim, California, born in a barn in 1909, falls right into the line of enthusiasts who were utterly fascinated by the new world of electronics and radio. An accountant by training but a tinkerer at heart—and a workaholic by preference—

Fender opened his Fender Radio Service in downtown Fullerton, California. This was the era when electric guitar meant a hollow-body archtop with a bar or horseshoe magnet pickup, and constant problems of feedback and twitchy technology. Fender's business card listed his interests: "electrical appliances, phonograph records, musical instruments & repairs, public address systems, sheet music."

Though not a player, Fender listened to guitarists and understood their problems, and it wasn't long before he rose to the challenge of solving them. He was the first to design a pickup using separate magnets for each string. Then came the next obvious challenge:

Fender Thinline Telecaster, 1972

Could one build a solid-body guitar, getting rid of the feedback inherent in hollow-body designs? Working with Doc Kaufmann, a professional lap-steel guitarist and former worker with the nearby Rickenbacker company, the two created a prototype electric solid-body guitar in 1943 and, after the war, they began manufacturing lap steels and amplifiers. By 1949, Fender designed the guitar that would become known the world over as the Fender Telecaster.

Like the Model T, the Telecaster (appearing first as the Broadcaster) was a masterpiece of simplicity and functionality.

Designed, also like the Model T, to be easily mass-produced, it consisted of a slab of ash, a screw-on neck, two knobs, and a pickup. Its one stylish flourish was the Stauffer-like headstock with tuning pegs all in a row.

Around the same time, Fender introduced a second instrument that would have an equally profound effect on modern music: the electric bass. Called the Precision Bass because of its frets (allowing players to hit precisely the right notes), it freed the bassist from the acoustic behemoth affectionately known as a "doghouse," and amplified the

Fender D'Aquisto, 1985

instrument's heartbeat. Add a set of drums, and you didn't need a big band to get the big sound.

Still listening to guitarists (including Fender employee Freddy Tavares, whose swooping guitar whoosh is known to anyone who's ever heard the opening of a Looney Tunes cartoon), Fender pulled off the trifecta of genius designs when he introduced the Stratocaster in 1954. Where the Telecaster's form seemed dictated by the demands of its function, the Stratocaster arrived as if out of the future. The two cutaways, the beveled body, an unheard-of three pickups with selector switches, and especially the self-contained vibrato unit: It was revolutionary. And it took more than a decade for a player to realize its full potential, in the hands of Jimi Hendrix.

With Buddy Holly featuring a Strat and more and more players turning to the new electric sound, Leo Fender's business grew by leaps and bounds. Yet by 1965, the somewhat hypochondriac genius was so worn down by a persistent strep infection, along with the financial burden of growing a business, that he arranged the sale of the company

Fender Bronco, 1978

to CBS. The price tag: an astonishing sum of \$13 million, \$2 million more than what they'd just paid for the New York Yankees.

Leo Fender continued on as a consultant to CBS. But once his noncompete contract expired, and a doctor cured his sinuses with a massive course of antibiotics, he joined Ernie Ball at Music Man, and later, with George Fullerton, founded G&L ("George and Leo," then after Fullerton left, "Guitars by Leo"). He died at his shop in 1991. A year later he was inducted into the Rock and Roll Hall of Fame.

SPOT THE CLONE

Tried and true, Telecasters are much the same as they were back in the early 1950s, when this well-used model with its smudged fretboard left the assembly line. Still, there's always room for tweaking: The brand-new Linhof Special, made by Kurt Linhof, is a tone monster with a Fralin split-coil humbucker in the neck position and a Fralin reverse-angled bridge pickup, which boosts the lead while removing the extreme ice-pick sound.

Kurt Linhof Special,
2006

Fender Telecaster,
1955

Gretsch "Bo Diddley"
Big B, 1960

Melobar, 1970s

SQUARED OFF

Hard to imagine anything less elegant than this rectangular plank, but of course it's instantly recognizable because one player—Bo Diddley—made it his trademark "Big B." On the other hand, lots of musicians, from Jimmy Page to Keith Richards to Bonnie Raitt, used a Melobar, a slide guitar that can be played standing up because of the way the neck is mounted at a 45-degree angle from the body. LaBaye stripped the guitar to its basics: pickups and strings mounted on a 2×4.

LaBaye 2 × 4 Six, 1967. 45 were built for NAMM, the industry's trade show, and LaBaye never received a single order.

SYMBOLIC

Looking like a menacing heavy metal ax, the Maltese Cross was made by a quirky luthier named Harvey Thomas. Years later, Ian Hunter of Mott the Hoople "endorsed" it after finding one in a pawnshop. This blond Gibson Flying V belonged to the man who put it on the map, Albert King. Surprise, surprise, the rhinestone star guitar used to be Paul Stanley's (of Kiss). On the headstock is an image of Stanley holding the guitar.

Thomas Maltese Cross, 1966

Gibson Flying V, 1980s, played by Albert King

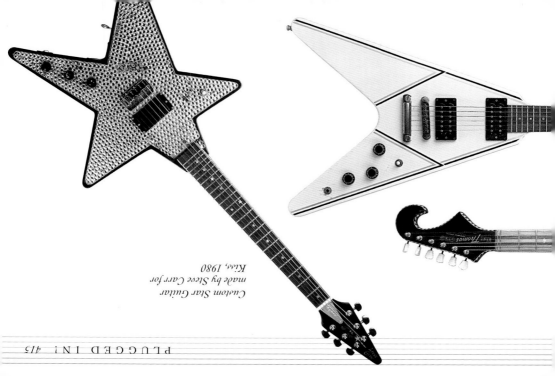

*Custom Star Guitar
made by Steve Carr for
Kiss, 1980*

MARTIN GOES ELECTRIC ... and no one cared. After generations of doing what it does better than anyone else, Martin tried, with a resounding lack of success, to join the electric boom. The DeArmond pickup cluttered the sound hole on this 00-18E; the big and, for Martin, flashy GT-75 was called a "treble bomb" by Junior Watson. In the late 1970s, Dick Boak made a few progressive solid-body prototypes, the Swan and Parabola—perhaps too progressive, as they never saw the factory floor.

Martin 00-18E, 1960

Martin GT-75, 1967

Dick Boak's Parabola (above) and Swan, both 1978

*Ovation Deacon, 1975,
the company's high-end
electric offering*

DEACON BLUES

Like Martin, Ovation could not translate
its one success—in creating the acoustic-
electric guitar—into another—the straight
electric guitar. It tried, though, with a
variety of models, including this Deacon,
one of the first American production guitars
that came with active onboard electronics.

GIRL POWER

The guitar world isn't totally awash in testosterone. Gretsch made a stab at reaching female players in 1962 with the Princess. Then along came Daisy Rock, founded by Tish Ciravalo, with guitars for women of every age, from the shapes that appeal to young girls to sophisticated retro instruments with their lighter bodies and thinner necks. They are played by an impressive roster of musicians.

Gretsch Princess, 1962

Daisy Rock Midnight Purple Burst, 2000s

Daisy Rock Candy Apple Pink, 2000s

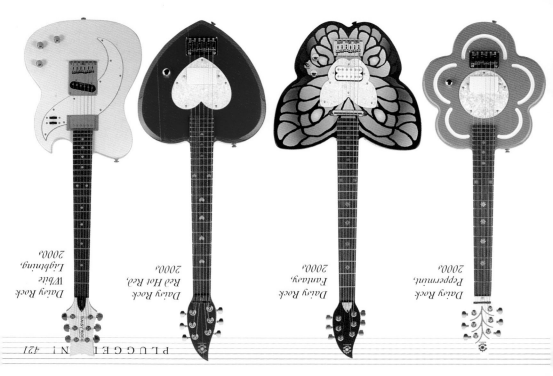

Daisy Rock,
White
Lightning,
2000.

Daisy Rock,
Red Hot Red,
2000.

Daisy Rock,
Fantasy,
2000.

Daisy Rock,
Peppermint,
2000.

WIRED

There's something about the electric guitar that appeals as much to the tinkerer as the musician. Micro-Frets, a company founded by an inventor named Ralph Jones, offered the first cordless guitar, the Orbiter, with an antenna and FM transmitter. From the Italian owners of Godwin came this guitar-organ with complicated controls. It featured wired frets so that contact with the strings completed a special circuit and opened up a world of sounds and sustain. All difficult to control.

Micro-Frets
Orbiter, 1968

Godwin guitar-organ, 1976

The Orbiter

Godwin ORGAN

"THAT GREAT GRETSCH SOUND"

A family company that made drums, banjos, and tambourines, Gretsch produced—and still sells—some of the most stylish, distinguished-sounding guitars. Its heyday was the 1950s and early '60s, when the company signed Chet Atkins, was the first to introduce automobile-style colors, explored dozens of different models, and outsold Fender. The good times climaxed when George Harrison played the famous Country Gentleman. As the years wore on, Gretsch found its niche as the preferred country-western and rockabilly guitar.

Gretsch Roundup 6130, 1954

Gretsch Chet Atkins 6120, 1957, in classic western orange finish

Gretsch Silver Jet, 1960s

Gretsch Tempo, 1960s

Gretsch Tennessean, 1967

ARTISAN ELECTRICS

No matter what the medium—archtop or flattop, acoustic or electric—a master-built instrument is a concrete expression of the luthier's philosophy. Tom Ribbecke's amazing attention to detail and tradition is visible even in a photograph of his 335-inspired semi-hollow electric—as is Harry Fleishman's passion for shaking things up and exploring new ideas.

Ribbecke Thin-line Electric, 1996

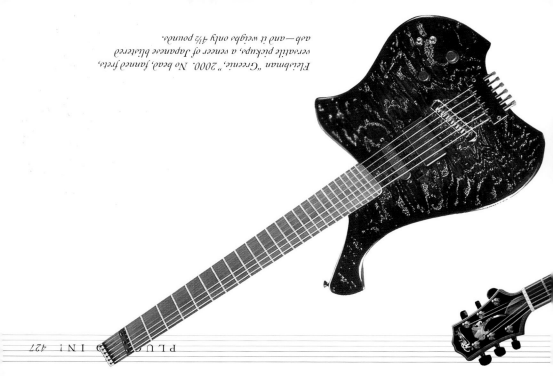

Fleishman "Greenie," 2000. No head, fanned frets, versatile pickups, a veneer of Japanese blistered ash—and it weighs only 4½ pounds.

THE FOX

Built to do it all, the Taylor T5—the company's first foray into the
electric guitar world—integrates both the acoustic and electric
guitars through its advanced electronics. Its potential is staggering.
Select from five positions, add voicing to each, plug it into an acoustic
amp or a Marshall stack.

Taylor T-5, 2000s

THE HEDGEHOG

In a cramped, one-man shop in Greenwich Village, Rick Kelly builds solid-body electric guitars. Everything about this guitar screams single-coil purity. But there's something very special about the wood: It's first-growth yellow pine from the ceiling of a Bowery loft, where it was aged by a century-and-a-half of scorching summer heat and bitter New York winter cold.

Kelly single pickup electric, 2007

Kramer Triaxe,
1986

Kawai M5-700 Moonsault, 1982. This is not the only time a guitar-maker used the crescent shape, but perhaps the only time it was done right, with the phases of the moon fingerboard decoration and silver-to-shade coloring that seems to glow.

SHAPELY

One looks like a rocket ship, the other like the moon it is speeding toward. The 1980s, in particular, released a lot of futuristic ideas in guitar designers. Plug in, and travel through time.

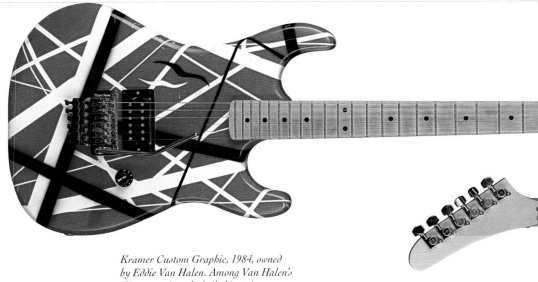

*Kramer Custom Graphic, 1984, owned
by Eddie Van Halen. Among Van Halen's
idiosyncrasies—he boils his strings
before using them.*

FAUX FRANKENSTRAT

One of the most famous modern guitars is Eddie Van Halen's "Frankenstrat,"
originally just black-and-white and built by Van Halen from a used neck and
imperfect body. Van Halen's goal was a Gibson sound with a Fender feel,
and one of its famous features is the single volume control. Kramer started
building guitars for Eddie in 1984.

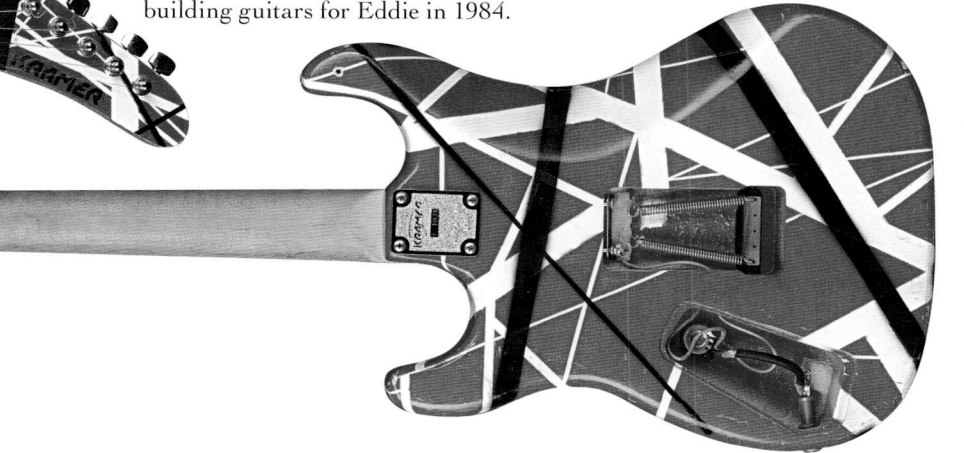

SIX

The Circle Turns

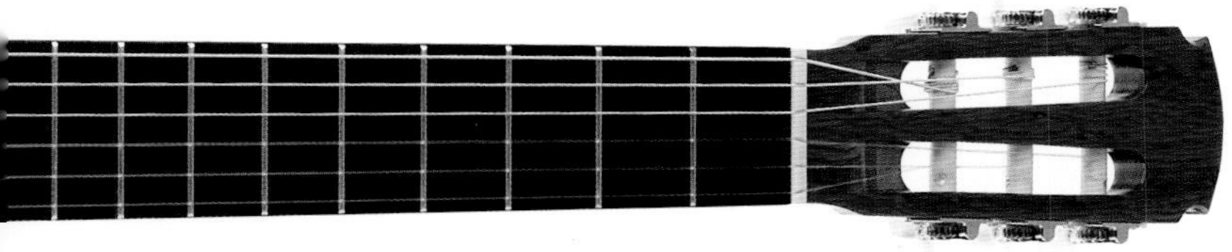

Jesse Carpenter, 2005

A New Golden Age

What a lucky time to be a guitar player. More than ever before, it's possible for a player to have exactly "his guitar" or "her guitar." To have the guitar that most says "you." A guitar that speaks to you, and through which you speak. A guitar that fits your body, your style, your personality, your every musical desire. And if one guitar alone can't satisfy you, well, there's another guitar out there for you. Maybe it's a Mike Greenfield or Tom Ribbecke custom-made archtop perfect for your jazz moods, or a Santa Cruz Firefly, the cute little travel guitar that fits in a plane's overhead. If it's a nylon-string guitar you're after, look to luthier Thomas Humphrey and his Millennium guitar.

Just like its biggest fans from the sixties, the guitar has finally grown up. Through players like Segovia and Django and Charlie Christian and Gene Autry, it stepped to the front of the stage, a beautiful, intriguing ingenue. And when Hendrix and Clapton and The Rolling Stones plugged in, it took over, the loudest adolescent in the room. But face it, it's an adult now. The electric guitar isn't

*Santa Cruz
Firefly, 2006*

dangerous anymore, and neither are the Stones. The funky, woodsy Gibson L-00 is now marketed as the "Blues King"—the name's embroidered on the gig bag! At your local Guitar Center, that cacophony of heavy-metal licks is as likely to come from a graying boomer as it is from a tattooed teenager.

But in another sense, the guitar has come full circle. As it rose in popularity, it left the workshops of artisans and became industrialized. But lately, a kind of anti-industry has formed, partly a revolution and partly a reaction. The guitar is back in the workshops again.

It started when players like Neil Young noticed "the magic in old guitars." His revelation came with a prewar Martin D-45. But how to explain it? Maybe the wood Martin used in the 1930s was, like the tonewoods that found their way into the workshops of Stradivari and Guarneri, just better-quality, dense first-growth red spruce conducive to producing uncannily beautiful sounds. Or maybe the lacquer, through the process of checking and stretching, released

Ribbecke
7-string 2000

its grip on the top. Or was it something mysterious, as if the very spruce molecules themselves, having been pushed around for half a century or more, finally lined up in exactly the right direction? Or did the craftsmen back then just *know* things that are no longer known?

So a few talented people who loved wood and music decided to figure things out. Some of them worked at the repair benches of guitar dealers, up to their elbows in prewar Ds and OMs. Others were musical do-it-yourselfers who grew more interested in making the box than making the sounds that came out of the box, and built their first guitars practically from scratch (in the days long before the Stewart-MacDonald catalog offered a soup-to-nuts collection of luthier supplies). They used the old Martins and Gibsons as paradigms, and sought to replicate what made them tick so soulfully.

Some pressed on and became luthiers. A luthier is a mixture of highly skilled craftsman, acoustic engineer, tree whisperer, and artist. Today there are something like 1,500 active luthiers, and

Grit Laskin
"6.0, 6.0," 2001

the most successful have waiting lists longer than it would take to go to Berklee and earn a BS in jazz guitar. They tap the planks of tone wood and hear its soul; forever experiment with the blizzard of minute details that go into making the guitar come alive; work out their own ideas about everything from the decoration of a heelcap to traditional vs. innovative bracing inside. And build guitars using little more than a penknife and their Torres-like fingers. Plus they offer the ultimate in

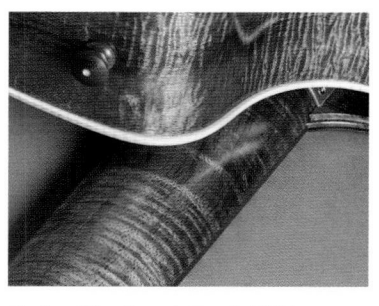

Parker Olive Branch, detail, 2006

consumer interaction: A player sits down with the builder, discusses sizes and shapes and styles of music, runs through a few best tunes while the luthier observes (this is where the performance-challenged or pure fantasist may prefer to work over the phone), and in a few months—or years, depending on the waiting list—he or she is the proud owner of a one-of-a-kind guitar.

Some combined their love for building guitars with an entrepreneurial spirit, turning passion and artistry into a company, albeit a comparatively small, personal company. It's what happened with makers like Richard Hoover at Santa Cruz and Bill Collings of Collings Guitar. The timing worked out well; these boutique makers found space to grow during a period when their big industry counterparts seemed to be faltering. And their innate appeal—just like a Martin or a Gibson, only *better*—started reaching an audience that was becoming more discerning by the day.

Some took it a step further, questioning not just what made a Martin or Gibson or D'Angelico work, but what made the guitar work. As conservative as much contemporary guitar design is—and really, nearly every guitar for sale at your local music store is either a Strat or a copy of a Strat, Tele or a copy of a Tele, Les Paul or copy, Martin or clone—there is always another restless, ingenious innovator out there who knows the guitar is a relatively young instrument, an instrument in flux from the moment it existed.

Rick Davis Running Dog "Big Dog Baritone," 2005

And he knows that by asking the right questions—in wood

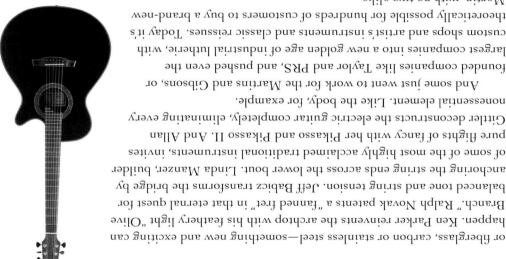

Charles Fox Ergo,
2005

or fiberglass, carbon or stainless steel—something new and exciting can happen. Ken Parker reinvents the archtop with his feathery light "Olive Branch." Ralph Novak patents a "fanned fret" in that eternal quest for balanced tone and string tension. Jeff Babicz transforms the bridge by anchoring the string ends across the lower bout. Linda Manzer, builder of some of the most highly acclaimed traditional instruments, invites pure flights of fancy with her Pikasso and Pikasso II. And Allan Gittler deconstructs the electric guitar completely, eliminating every nonessential element. Like the body, for example.

And some just went to work for the Martins and Gibsons, or founded companies like Taylor and PRS, and pushed even the largest companies into a new golden age of industrial lutherie, with custom shops and artist's instruments and classic reissues. Today it's theoretically possible for hundreds of customers to buy a brand-new Martin, with no two alike.

Which one will you take?

*Norman Forbidden
Fruit 12-string
Resonator, 2005*

NEW OLD

Paul Norman, a self-styled Renaissance man, presents the perfect blues guitar: A 12-string resonator that can be heard in the noisiest joint. Harking back to the Weissenborn guitars of the 1920s, this Kona Hawaiian Model steel guitar comes from Bear Creek Guitars in Maui. With its shimmering curly koa and ropelike trim, it was custom-made for the guitarist Bob Brozman.

Bear Creek Guitars
Custom Kona, 2005

*Santa Cruz mahogany-bodied
H-13, 2006*

THE ONE

Inspired by Gibson's 1928 Nick Lucas, the Santa Cruz
H-13 is one of those rare steel-strings built to do it
all. With its deep body, uncommon 13-fret neck joint,
enlarged sound hole, and typical Santa Cruz attention
to balanced tone and detail, this is a small-bodied fingerstyle instrument that turns into a sound cannon when
you drive it hard. And what a looker.

Richard Hoover and the Santa Cruz Guitar Company

Considering his location in Santa Cruz, California, surfing is a pretty good metaphor to describe how Richard Hoover has ridden the wave of interest in high-quality steel-string guitars that started in the late 1960s, and grew and grew and grew. He had his epiphany quite young. Soon after he learned to play the guitar, he stepped back, looked at it through different eyes, and realized it had actually been *made* by someone. And that someone could be him. A second and more complex epiphany came later: In the course of becoming a luthier, he understood that while he had the vision to create the very finest guitars for the players of his generation, he didn't have the patience to get there by painstakingly building them one at a time. Thus he developed the boutique guitar concept, where a small group of highly skilled craftsmen can produce a line of exemplary instruments.

It's all about the woods, the people, and the marriage of tradition and innovation. Things that need to be done by expert hand—choosing the tonewoods, tuning the braces—are done by hand. The most professional of computer-

controlled tools are employed for precise but repetitive tasks, like carving consistent bridges out of ebony. Hoover and his gifted crew (alumni include Jeff Traugott and Bill Hardin), obsess over every detail. The bodies are light and slightly rounded, more like a naturally strong egg than a rigid box. The nitrocellulose finish breathes and is repairable. Headstocks and joints are designed to either let the sound rise up the neck like a chimney, enveloping the player, or focus it forward. And the goal is always to imbue each guitar with the nonsubjective benchmarks of sound: sustain, overtones, richness.

Santa Cruz archtop, 2007

*Mark Lacey Blue
Marlin archtop,
2000s*

*Michael Hemken
archtop, 2005*

ARCHTOP RENAISSANCE

Though Charlie Christian's electric pickup appeared to sound a long death knell for the acoustic archtop, its beauty, unexpected versatility, and inherent challenge proved irresistible to luthiers. It's still a serious instrument for serious players (with a serious price tag), and enough builders are drawn to the form to keep it vital.

PAIR OF BOZOS—pronounced *Bo-Zhos*. A Serbian master luthier, Bozo Podunavac emigrated to the U.S. and started building his own guitars in Chicago in 1964. His instruments shimmer with pearl and abalone and are known for their rich tone and sustain. The Requinto follows Podunavac's unique Bell Western template (like a dreadnought, but with a larger lower bout and smaller, square upper bout). By the way, a "requinto guitar" is a small-bodied acoustic lead guitar in a mariachi band. Notice that the neck joins the body at the 16th fret. The Chicagoan was built for the Scott Chinery Blue Guitar project.

Bozo Requinto,
1996

Bozo Chicagoan,
1996

SEARCH FOR QUALITY

Whether looking back or looking forward, contemporary lutherie is always about finding the highest expression of the instrument. Shelley D. Park creates a hybrid of two original Selmer/Maccaferri designs with her Avance d-hole gypsy guitar. Valentino Lamorte's Folk Slim brings together the builder's experience with electric and acoustic guitar-making. Aiming for a fully energized soundboard, Jeff Babicz anchors the individual strings across the lower bout. With a name that translates into "tree craftsman," and with a grandmother named D'Addario (of the string family), what better career could Fabrizio Alberico pursue than lutherie?

*Shelley D. Park
Modèle Avance,
2005*

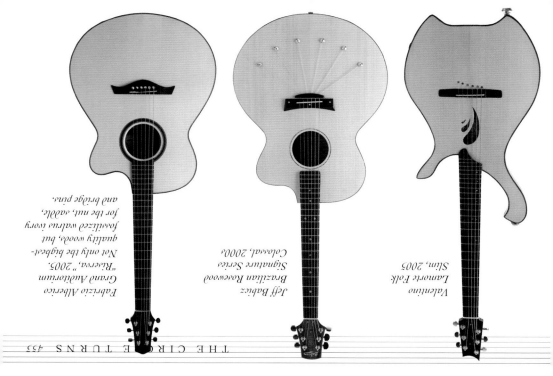

Fabrizio Alberico
Grand Auditorium
"Riserva," 2005.
Not only the highest-
quality woods, but
fossilized walrus ivory
for the nut, saddle,
and bridge pins.

Jeff Babicz
Brazilian Rosewood
Signature Series
Colossal, 2005.

Valentino Lamorte
Folk
Slim, 2005

JUST 12 guitars a year. That's the output of Michael Greenfield, a Montreal luthier who refuses to distinguish between "standard" and "deluxe." Same with labels like "traditional" or "innovative." He may use the hot, animal-hide glue that's been the choice of instrument makers for centuries, but he's using it to create some fairly radical instruments.

Michael Greenfield Changui, 2005, with an extra bass string and unusual 29"–25" scale length.

Michael Greenfield Brahms, 2007. A classical meets the Novax fanned fret system meets two extra strings—low A on the bass and high A on the treble.

ON EVERY PLAYER'S MIND

Custom luthier Howard
Klepper plays with one
of the oldest clichés about
the guitar, turning it
into a sculpture that's
also a whimsical visual
joke. Oh, and the joke
continues on the backside
of Nakyd Laydie.

Howard Klepper
Nakyd Laydie, 2005

Giannini Craviola CRA6S, 1970

"EXOTIC GENIUS"

Founded by classical luthier Tranquilo Giannini at the turn of the 20th century, the Giannini company is one of the biggest names in Latin American guitars. During the folk boom, it began exporting steel-string models to the U.S., including the asymmetrical Craviola. Ads for it touted its "deeper, more penetrating clearer sound," "great playing comfort," and "mellow tone from within rare Brazilian rosewood walls," all created with "a stroke of exotic genius."

HARP-GUITARS

For years you'd see them in guitar stores, high up on the wall, gathering dust, exotic harp-guitars from another century. Now, with the revival of lutherie, comes a new breed of harp-guitars— and players who utilize those extra bass strings to create music with incredible range and depth.

Duane Noble harp-guitar, 2005 (front and back)

Mark Deering Autumn harp-guitar, 2000s

Fred Carlson Big Red, harp-sympitar, 2005. The swirling, colorful back (right) is cast from recycled paper grocery bags.

ENOUGH STRINGS?

Luthier Jamie Kinscherff fashions
a 12-string with quilted mahogany
body and a top of bear-claw Sitka
spruce (see the shimmer in the
top). He even includes a cutaway,
uncommon for a 12-string, to
tempt players to the higher frets.
Moonstone's double-neck of 6 and
12 strings is a large-bodied Brazilian;
both necks share a piece of the wide
oval sound hole. With 42 tunable
strings going every which way, the
aptly named Pikasso II is the guitar
as sculpture, a museum-quality
piece built by Linda Manzer with
design inspiration from a favorite
player of her guitars, Pat Metheny.

*Jamie Kinscherff
High Noon 12-C,
2005*

*Moonstone Guitars
J99 Double-Neck
Brazilian, 2005*

Linda Manzer Pikasso II, 1995

MUSICAL SCULPTURE

Playful, sophisticated, idiosyncratic, this Bauhaus guitar reflects the life of the man who built it, Jean Weinfeld, who worked on the first kibbutzim in Palestine in the 1920s, studied with Mies van der Rohe and Paul Klee at the Bauhaus in the early 1930s, was imprisoned by the Nazis in Paris during World War II, and then, postwar, resumed his architectural career. He also had a lifelong fascination for musical instruments and created dozens of fanciful guitar sculptures. Though the "sound holes" look oddly convincing, the Bauhaus guitar doesn't actually make music.

*Bauhaus guitar,
1960*

ART GALLERY

Hand in hand with the new wave of lutherie
is a new art of inlay. Perhaps its most notable
practitioner is William "Grit" Laskin, who
wields his #6 Onglette engraver like the
finest sable brush on headstocks, sound holes,
fretboards—and anywhere else possible.
Here's a Laskin sampler.

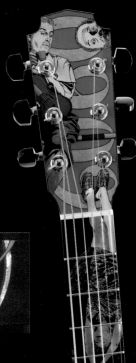

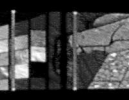
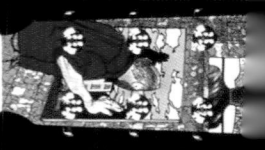

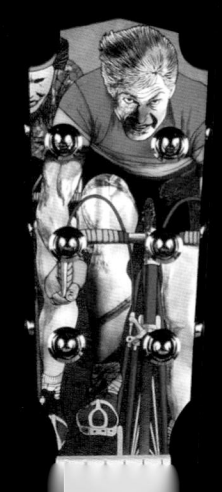
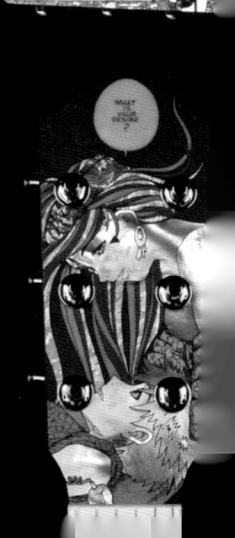

Humphrey
Millennium, 1987

ARTIST MEETING ARTIST

Thomas Humphrey not only experimented with the neck angle and fingerboard when creating his important Millennium guitar, but, as this model attests, he tried other unconventional touches, like the F-holes in the upper bout and the decorative scroll on the headstock. He also works with an artist, Tamara Codor, who paints the backs and sides of select Humphrey guitars, giving them a secret, romantic identity.

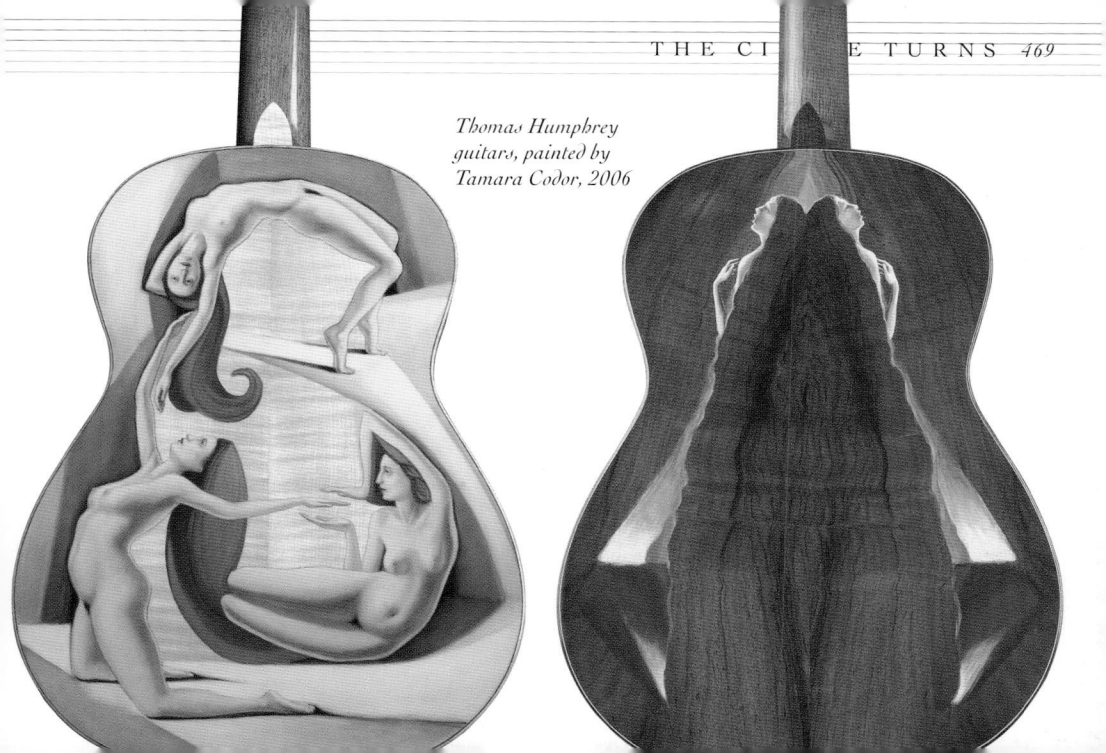

*Thomas Humphrey
guitars, painted by
Tamara Codor, 2006*

WHAT WOULD TORRES THINK?

In experimenting with the classical guitar, two builders take sideways leaps: Jesse Carpenter's is in-your-face, with its off-center sound hole and series of cutaways. Master steel-string builder Ed Claxton tries something more subtle but tonally just as startling: The top three strings of his very traditional-looking classical guitar are steel instead of nylon—one can only imagine the richness of the bright-on-top, mellow-on-bottom contrast.

Jesse Carpenter cutaway classical, 2005

Ed Claxton classical steel-string, 2000s (front and back)

GREATS *Sharon Isbin*

She's been compared to Monet in her range of coloristic effects. The guitar in her hands, a reviewer once wrote, takes on the precision of a diamond, every note a facet that is clear, polished, shining. Isbin gets right to the heart of the guitar's intimate nature: "There are no keys, there's no bow . . . you literally caress the instrument and the strings," she says. It was her brother who was supposed to take the guitar lessons while the family sojourned in Italy, but the nine-year-old Sharon started instead and never looked back. She studied with Segovia, founded the classical guitar department at Juilliard (and became its first professor), and won back-to-back Grammies, in 2001 and 2002, the first solo guitarist to do so in 30 years. She also works hard on the issue facing every classical musician: how to keep relevant in an age that seems less and less interested in classical music. Her solution is to expand the repertoire—to step outside the classical idiom, playing and recording everything from folk ("Dreams of a World") to film scores (*The Departed*) to crossover, performing with rock guitarist Steve Vai on his composition "Blossom Street," to original compositions written expressly for her, like John Duarte's "Joan Baez Suite."

Mike Greenfield, The Phoenix, 2007

BIG CELEBRATIONS, PART I

In the spring of 2007, Mike Greenfield built his 100th acoustic guitar. He writes: "To celebrate this milestone, I decided to use an exceptional piece of very old and very rare bear-claw western red cedar which I had been saving for many years. Now clear your mind and imagine the rich, dulcet chime of the Dalai Lama's wooden bell, suspended from a golden thread . . . and that's just the tap-tone!"

The Phoenix also features quilted mahogany back and sides and a very old, perfectly straight-grained and quarter-sawn true Honduran mahogany neck.

Santa Cruz Nouveau, 2007
(front and back)

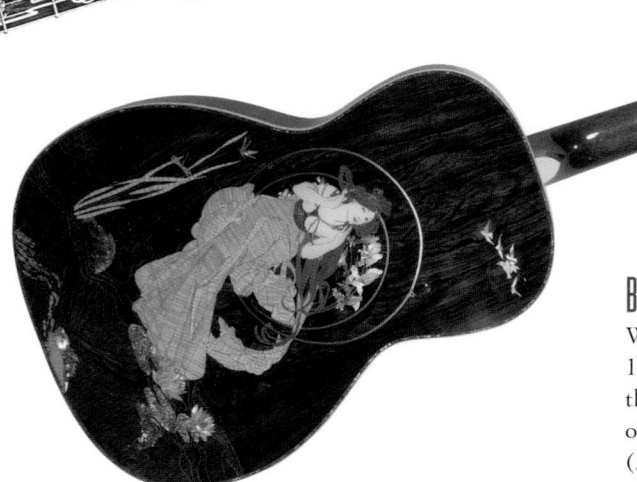

BIG CELEBRATIONS, PART II

With 30 years in business and 10,000 guitars, Santa Cruz created the Nouveau, a stunning melange of inlay (Larry Robinson), painting (Michael Coy), and details, like the silver spiderweb rosette.

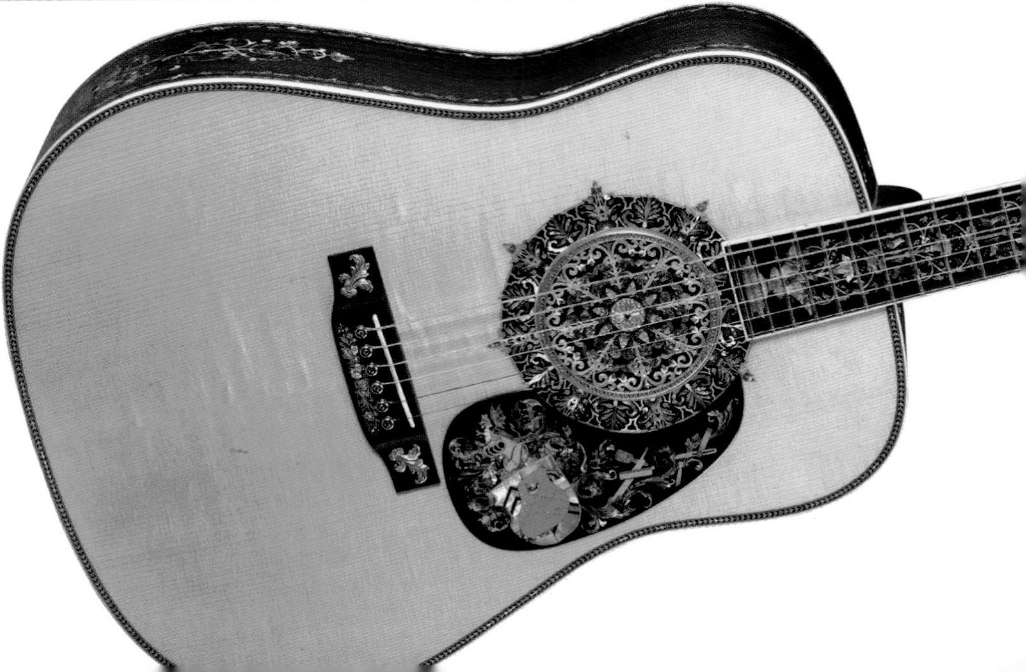

BIG CELEBRATIONS, PART III

#1,000,000. It's the most elaborate guitar in Martin's history, featuring Baroque- and Victorian-themed inlays of abalone, mother-of-pearl, sea snail, 18-karat gold, white gold, and precious gems, including diamonds, emeralds, rubies, sapphires, and aquamarines. It's a dreadnought, of course, and it represents 171 years of musical history.

Martin Millionth
Guitar, unveiled in 2005
(front and back)

A MILLION GUITARS LATER,

Martin can play, as evidenced by the irreverent figure of Felix on this model. Some children are born with a silver spoon in their mouth. But when you're a Martin, it's only fitting to get a custom guitar. Claire's Guitar (the seventh-generation C. F. Martin) is an elegant three-quarter-size pink guitar with, most endearingly, the initials C.F.M. in baby-block inlay on the fretboard.

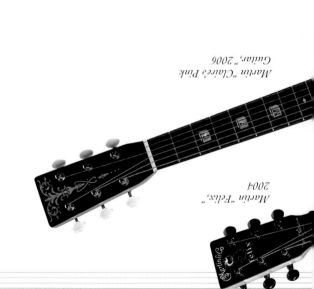

Martin "Claire's Pink Guitar," 2006

Martin "Felix," 2004

GREATS *Eric Clapton*

Struggling guitarists, take note: The story has it that after receiving his first guitar at the age of 13, Eric Clapton found the instrument so difficult to learn that he just about gave up. Instead, like all teenage rock-stars-in-training, Clapton spent hours in his room laboring to play along with recordings, in his case music by the likes of Big Bill Broonzy and Muddy Waters. He carried his passion for blues, and his superior technique, first to The Yardbirds and then to John Mayall and the Bluesbreakers, where the 21-year-old's electrifying solos inspired the slogan *Clapton is God* to appear on a wall in the London Underground. Bends, trills, powerful riffs, vibrato, hammer-ons and pull-offs, distortion—Clapton could do it all, and with innate tastefulness, control, and a sublime sense of tension and release. After the Bluesbreakers came a succession of supergroups, including Cream and Derek and the Dominos. Then, for many fans, perhaps *the* defining moment in a career of milestones: the *MTV Unplugged* concert and recording, which showed just how far Clapton had evolved from a British guitar hero into a complete artist, fusing instrument, voice, and songwriting talents.

BLACK & WHITE

The collaboration between Martin and Eric Clapton has been a hit; the artist's signature 000-28EC is so successful, it moved from custom edition to stock model. In 2004, Martin and Clapton added a third party to the mix, Japanese designer and trendsetter Hiroshi Fujiwara, creating the stunning Bellezza Nera ("Black Beauty"), then its sister, Bellezza Bianca ("White Beauty"). By the way, Martin's first-ever guitar finished in black was a D-35 made for Johnny Cash.

*Martin
Bellezza
Bianca, 2004*

*Martin
Bellezza
Nera, 2004*

DYLAN-ESQUE

Bob Dylan has clearly never felt the need or the desire to endorse a guitar, but when he saw the prototype HDN Negative Martin created for the 10th-anniversary edition of *Acoustic Guitar*, he sent out word that he wanted one. His came with two matching pickguards, and fans often saw him play it while on the Neverending Tour after *Love & Theft*.

HDN "Negative" Martin," 2000. Note the black bridge and nut.

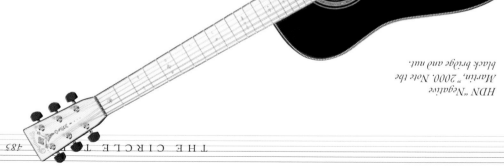

FANNED FRETS

The typical guitar fretboard is a study in right angles. But the geometry of a player's hand is not so rigid, nor should all strings on a guitar be the same length; otherwise there are intonation problems. A fanned fret system, designed (and patented) by luthier Ralph Novak, gives each string its own scale length and matches the fretboard angle with the arc of the player's hand. Proponents say it creates a richer, clearer sound, particularly on the lower strings.

Paul Davis Snake Head, 2005

Jeff Traugott Model R Fan Fret, 2005 — the builder's personal guitar

ALL-IN-ONE

Built by Jeff Traugott, this fanned fret, seven-string electric guitar was custom-made for Charlie Hunter, a contemporary phenom who plays lead guitar (on the top strings) and bass guitar (on the bottom strings) simultaneously. The futuristic-looking disks are actually pickup covers.

Jeff Traugott's Charlie Hunter electric, 2006

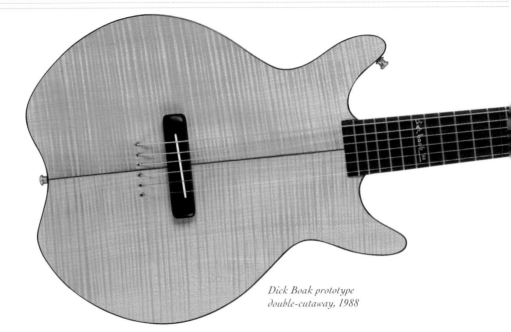

*Dick Boak prototype
double-cutaway, 1988*

IS THERE ANYONE ELSE in the contemporary guitar world like

Dick Boak, artist, author, marketing genius (for Martin), sometime musician, curator, innovator, and luthier? This double-cutaway is Boak's prototype for a thin-bodied electric guitar meant to appeal to acoustic players as well, using an acoustic Fishman Thinline bridge pickup. It joins Boak's other full-on electrics (see pages 416–17) that Martin never put into production.

TOUCHY-FEELY

This mad scientist special goes beyond
guitar basics—fretting and strumming—
to create a whole new way of playing:
You tap the strings like piano keys. It
was invented in 1955 by a 21-year-old
named Dave Bunker, who unveiled his
Duo-Lectar Touch Guitar in 1960 on the
national television show *Jubilee U.S.A.*,
accompanying child singer Barbara
Mandrell. Leo Fender offered Bunker
$20,000 and a cut for the rights to make it.
Bunker turned him down, and continued to
develop patented ideas in his garage—for
muting the strings, for a guitar with tuning
pegs on its body, for innovative neck and
bridge designs—that he never quite knew
how to bring to market.

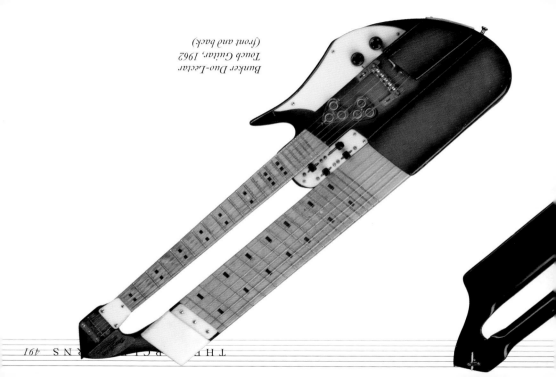

Bunker Duo-Lectar
Touch Guitar, 1962
(front and back)

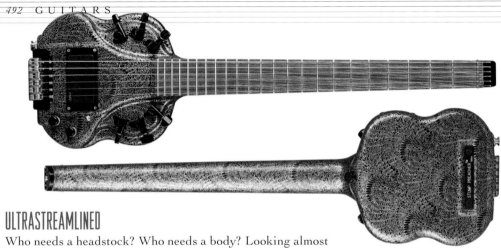

ULTRASTREAMLINED

Who needs a headstock? Who needs a body? Looking almost conventional in this crowd, the Stump Preacher prototype has a composite body whose back pops off for easy access to the strings and electronics. The Chapman Stick (lower right) looks like a guitar neck missing its body; it's meant to be tapped and/or fretted by both hands rather than plucked or strummed.

Stump Preacher prototype, 1996

SPACE-AGE

Through and through, the Gittler is the logical conclusion of what's left when everything inessential is removed from the solid-body electric guitar.

Gittler electric guitar, 1987

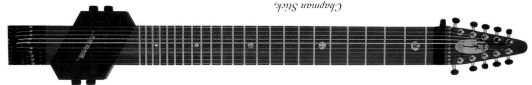

Chapman Stick, 1970s

Martin Backpacker,®
early 1990s

SPACE GUITAR—LITERALLY

The Martin Backpacker® has traveled and been
played everywhere, from the space shuttle to base
camp on Mt. Everest to Antarctica and the North
Pole. The design is radically clever, allowing this
rugged little instrument to produce a decent tone, rich
and loud. And the 24" scale means the fretboard is
comfortably close to a full-size guitar.

The Manzer, c. 2000. "This is the best acoustic guitar I have ever played."—Pat Metheny

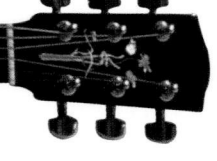

LINDA MANZER promises that if you've never owned a handmade guitar before, you are "in for an acoustical treat." After 25 years of making guitars, she celebrated with her own acoustical treat—The Bear, named after the use of "bear claw" spruce, an occasional feature found in spruce trees where it appears as if the wood had been gouged by a bear's claw.

Linda Manzer, The Bear, c. 1999. Note the "spirit" bear inlay on the headstock.

Linda Manzer

Sometimes one masterpiece is all it takes to make an artist's reputation. Linda Manzer's Pikasso (see page 463), the unforgettable arms-akimbo instrument whose 42 strings, when tuned, subject its innocent guitar body to 1,000 pounds of pressure, is a milestone of luthier creativity. But the fact is that Manzer was able to build it in collaboration with Pat Metheny because her regular old Manzer flattop— what Metheny calls the Linda-6—is such an amazing piece of work, capturing that holy grail of pianolike sound where the tones are balanced from the deepest bass to the highest treble. A student of both Jean-Claude Larivee, a sort of Canadian godfather of guitar-making, and James D'Aquisto, Linda Manzer brought a guitar to Metheny backstage after a concert in Toronto in 1982—and he's been using her guitars ever since. So have Bruce Cockburn, Carlos Santana, Milton Nascimento, Gordon Lightfoot, and Larry Campbell, among others.

Building guitars is like a puzzle, she once said, calling herself a "snazzy carpenter." She will build guitars of any shape and size, including miniature instruments like the 12-string Tiple, and is equally adept—and interested—in archtops and flattops, steel string and classical. A major innovation is her Wedge, a tapered body design wherein the bass side is narrower than the treble side. Like the scooped back of a Stratocaster, it brings the upper part of the guitar closer to the player's body, reducing strain on the strumming arm and giving the player a better view of the fretboard. But it's not all about innovation. "The most important thing to me," writes Manzer, "is that the player is inspired by the guitar. And plays it."

Linda Manzer 12-string Tiple, date unknown, her take on a small guitarlike chordophone used in South America

WHAT IS IT ABOUT THOSE ARCHTOPS?

Years after their heyday, archtop
guitars continue to preoccupy the
most obsessive and innovative
luthiers. Tom Ribbecke of northern
California builds them both
traditional—like this stunning green
guitar with classic f-holes—and
innovative—he's recently founded
a company to develop this
Halfling concept with its
unusual adjustable sound hole.

Ribbecke green archtop, 1995

Note the louvered sound hole on the upper bass bout.

Ribbecke Halfling, 2002. The bass side is constructed like a flattop, and the treble side like an archtop.

DUET

In what is surely a first, a luthier jam session, Tom Ribbecke and Linda Manzer built this guitar during a seven-day intensive workshop in Healdsburg, California, for an audience of fellow guitar-makers.

Tom Ribbecke and Linda Manzer, Duet, 2001

SPLIT PERSONALITY

The luthier Ken Parker claims that a successful guitar is an instrument in agreement with itself. Howard Klepper made the internal agreement of this instrument very clear, and permanent, zipping it together with dovetail joints—perhaps also a sly reference to the fabled neck joint of Martin guitars.

Howard Klepper, Dovetail Madness, 2000s, featuring 11 different woods

TWO-TONE

Literally—in color, but also sonically, with warmer cedar for the bass side and brighter spruce for the treble. These two are from Harry Fleishman, who makes every part of the guitar his own, from the intricate inlay and unusual bridges to creating a whole line of Asymmetrics.

Harry Fleishman Leona, 1990.
Note the individual bone saddle
for each string.

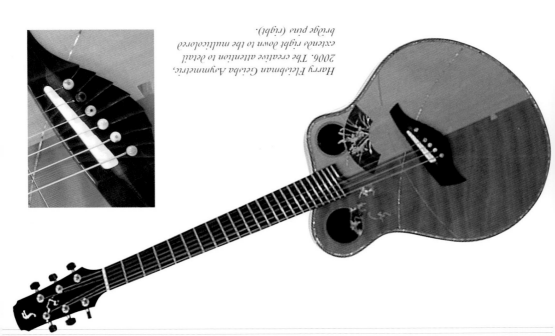

Harry Fleishman Geiaba Asymmetric, 2006. The creative attention to detail extends right down to the multicolored bridge pins (right).

Ken Parker

Some luthiers look back to the mythical golden age—Martins from before World War II, Gibsons of the Lloyd Loar era, the elegant Larsons and Washburns, freshly minted Fenders of the 1950s—and ask how, and re-create these splendid instruments with meticulous craftsmanship. Ken Parker, on the other hand, asks why. His wonderings and questions about electric solid-body guitars—why are they so heavy; why are they still made the same way they were 50 years ago; why, when you put one on your lap and let go, does it tip to the floor, with the headstock smacking you in the face?—led to the Parker Fly, the radically light, versatile, resonant guitar made of wood coated in fiberglass and carbon fiber, and using coil and piezo pickups for an incredible range of sound. After selling Parker Guitars to Washburn, who still makes the Fly, Parker retreated to upstate New York to return to an earlier obsession— the archtop guitar—and began a second round of "whys."

Parker Post-Fly electric, 2000s

The Olive Branch (see page 509) is the archtop guitar, radically reinvented. Like the Fly, it is born out of the passion of an artist who turns the familiar upside down and delivers a statement of startling originality. And who is so far ahead of the rest of the world that his invention only tantalizes— because it may be years, or never, before the average guitar-lover hears one, let alone plays one. Or maybe his ideas will trickle down. Maybe all guitars will one day be lighter, and, for want of a better word, "righter," built not with

indifference but guided by Parker's ethos of questioning every detail and never losing sight of the goal: "Listening is the end, and listening is the beginning."

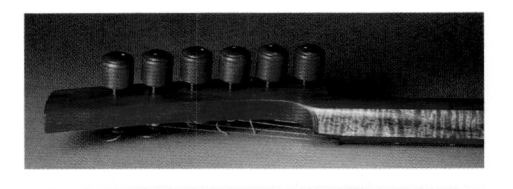

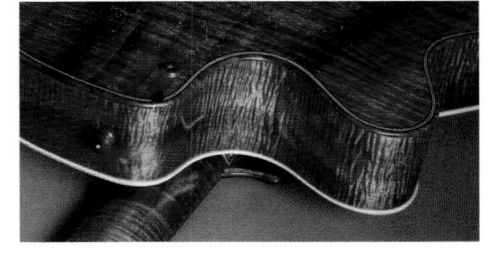

*Parker Olive
Branch, 2006*

ARCHTOP MADE NEW

Weighing in at an amazingly light three and a half pounds, the Olive Branch is luthier Ken Parker's return to his first love, the acoustic archtop guitar, and his attempt to mine the full potential of this misunderstood instrument. Is it a jazz guitar? Absolutely, for both soloing and comping. But it's also a guitar for fingerstyle, for funk, for flamenco—for everything. The top is red spruce, the back and sides Cocobolo, the sound hole a mere comma, and the tailpiece anodized aluminum. The string height can be adjusted by a hidden screw that elevates the neck.

POSTMODERN

German luthier Ulrich Teuffel seeks new answers for musical needs.
The Tesla is a 7-string guitar built for industrial music. It has an
extremely fat tone yet is capable of producing the ice-pick
sounds of an early Telecaster. The Birdfish puts
tone at the player's disposal. The two bars on
the left of the "body" are interchangeable
resonators; the pickups are
switchable and twistable; and
the control box on the lower
right controls volume, tone,
and input. Then swap out
the bridge and electronics,
plug in a MIDI box, and
voilà, a MIDI Birdfish.

*Teuffel Tesla
Standard, c. 2006*

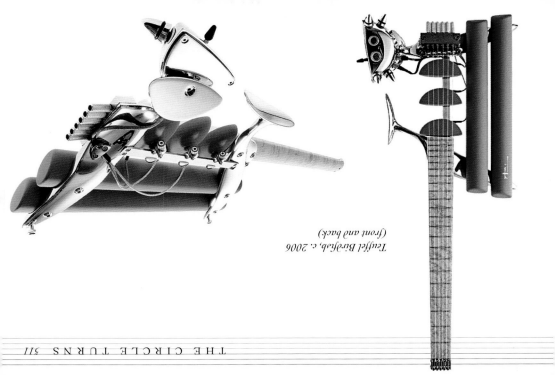

Teuffel Birdfish, c. 2006
(front and back)

*Chrysalis acoustic-
electric guitar, 1999*

PUNK AND POSTPUNK

Looking like something out of *The Matrix*, the acoustic-electric Chrysalis guitar was actually created by an inventor who studied insect aerodynamics in college—and discovered that the wing of a flying insect moves air as efficiently as a guitar top. The frame is made of graphite, the "body" is a fabric shell over an inflatable Mylar balloon, and the whole thing folds up to fit into a briefcase. This skateboard guitar from 1983 is a perfect intersection of subcultures. Fittingly, the neck is from an old Norma guitar, one of the cheapest builders of the '60s.

Skateboard guitar, 1983 (front and back)

CUTTING EDGE

Guitars have always been about embracing technology, whether using cutting-edge tools to create elaborate parchment rosettes in the 17th century, or plugging in electromagnetic pickups in the 20th. Here is a real glimpse of the future—the digital Les Paul.

Gibson HD.6X Pro Les Paul, 2007, with box pickup, which sends a separate signal for each string, giving unlimited freedom for digitally mixing, matching, blending, and distorting every sound the guitar produces

Very special thanks from the top to Leora Kahn, who acted as much as a partner in this project as a photo researcher. Though at one time she thought that all guitars looked alike, somewhere along the way—perhaps working all day in a dusty basement, helping to set up one after the other for the photo shoot—she discovered their individual beauty, and brought even more enthusiasm to the book. This project would never have gotten off the ground without her. Very, very special thanks, too, to Ruth Sullivan, not only because of her gift for putting together a book and drawing out an author's best, but because she rose to the occasion of an impossible schedule. And thank you to Sofia Tome and Maisie Tivnan—your hard work is greatly appreciated—and to Ellen Nygaard, who got it immediately, and to everyone at Workman: Janet Vicario, Susie Bolotin, Wayne Kirn, Melanie Bennitt, Anne Kerman, David Matt, Munira Al-Khalili, Pete Bohan, Justin Nisbet, Walter Weintz, James Wehrle, and, as always, Paul and Peter.

Turns out that the pleasure of guitars is not confined to the music—without exception, guitar collectors, guitar lovers, guitar makers, and guitar sellers are a singularly generous group. This book would not have been possible without their help: David Arky; Dave Belzer, known throughout the community as one of the two Burst Brothers, and Mike Catterino, his and our liaison at the Guitar Center's vintage shop; Dick Boak at Martin; Thomas Brunnell; Walter Carter for his tip about "Lucille"; Tish Ciravolo and Amber Chamberlain at Daisy Rock; Tamara Codor; Harry Fleishman; Kira Florita at the Country Music Hall of Fame and Museum; Frank Ford; Caroline Galloway and J. D. Schenk at Gibson; Mike Greenfield; Richard Hoover and Ronit Taggart and the staff at the Santa Cruz Guitar Company; Thomas Humphrey; Rick Kelly from Carmine Street Guitars; Grit Laskin; Buzz Levine and Lark Street Music; Jacob McMurray and the Experience Museum Project in Seattle; Beverly Maher, who runs the unique Guitar Salon in the heart of Greenwich Village; Linda Manzer; Fred Oster, who opened the doors to his extraordinary collection of prewar instruments; Ken Parker; Olivier Pozman; Tom Ribbecke; Juha Ruokangas; John Rydall; Mike Saccoliti and Steve Uhrik at Retrofret; Ulrich Teuffel; John Thomas; Jeff Traugott; and Stan Werbin and Dave Matchette from Elderly Instruments.

I also want to thank a great guitarist and teacher, Larry Maltz, and two lifelong guitar heroes, Bill Carr and John Reese. And especially, Asa, Quinn, Theo, and Clara, for everything.

CREDITS

Antonio de Torres Jurado: 264; Autry National Center: 52, 90; Biblioteca Nacional de España: 245; Carl Tremblay: 3, 10, 254, 256, 257 (top & bottom), 260-261, 344 (left), 352 (left), 375, 383 (bottom), 430-431 (top), 493 (both), 512; Carmine Street Guitars: 429; Collection Musée de la Musique (photos by Jean-Marc Anglés): 241, 246, 248 (both), 249, 253, 268; Corbis: 272; Country Music Hall of Fame: 14, 60 (right), 84 (2nd right), 85 (left), 91, 103, 121, 173, 174, 182-183 (2nd & 11th from left), 186-187, 204-205, 399 (left); Daisy Rock Guitars: 339, 420 (middle & right), 421 (all); David Arky: 29, 46 (both), 47 (middle & right), 48-49, 75, 104 (right), 118 (left), 119 (middle), 133 (both), 137 (left), 193, 208-209, 239, 294, 295 (left), 300, 303 (both), 304-305 (bottom), 310-311 (top), 312 (left), 316 (all), 317 (all), 325 (left, 2nd from left, right), 343 (left), 346 (right), 361 (left & middle), 368 (left), 377, 378 (left), 383 (top), 410-411 (bottom & top), 416 (left), 424 (left); Delta Haz Corporation: 86; Elderly Instruments: 6, 30, 31, 104 (left), 135, 146, 147, 152-153, 154 (bottom), 190-191, 297 (top), 299, 333, 334, 376 (bottom), 388 (right), 397 (middle), 401 (top); Experience Music Project: 2, 11, 24, 58, 59 (both), 60 (left), 74, 84 (left), 88, 89, 109, 115 (both), 124, 126, 127 (both), 134 (right), 136, 140-141, 143 (both), 148-149, 150, 151, 154 (top), 156-157, 158, 159, 160-161, 164, 166 (both), 169, 170 (bottom), 180-181, 182-183 (14th from left), 221-222, 237, 258 (left), 298 (top), 340 (left), 341 (both), 347, 348 (both), 349 (both), 356 (top), 357, 360 (left), 362 (right), 374 (right), 384 (both), 385, 393, 396 (right), 398 (left), 412 (top), 414 (both), 415, 432-433 (both), 490-491 (both), 492 (both), 513 (both); Fleishman Instruments: 427, 504, 505 (both); Frank Ford: 38 (right), 39, 84 (2nd from left), 139; Getty Images: 62, 76, 122, 128, 162, 178, 284, 285, 308, 354, 390, 406, 482; Gibson Guitars: 114, 392, 514-515; Greenfield Guitars: 232, 328, 329, 454, 455 (both), 474-475 (both); Guitar Salon International: 111, 265, 266, 269, 271, 275, 279, 280 (all), 281 (all), 283, 287, 288 (all); Jawbone Press: iii, v, 1, 4, 22, 26, 28, 40 (both), 43 (both), 44, 45, 47 (left), 50-51, 54 (right), 55, 56, 57, 64 (left & middle), 65 (both), 68, 69, 70 (right), 71 (both), 73, 82 (top), 85 (right), 93, 94, 95, 98-99, 100, 102, 106, 107 (both), 108 (left), 117, 119 (right), 130, 132, 138, 142, 182-183 (1st, 5th, 7th, 10th, 20th, 23rd from left); 184-185, 190, 194-195, 196-197,

198-199, 200-201, 202-203, 206-207, 212-213, 222-223, 226-227, 228-229, 251, 258 (right), 259 (both), 278, 282, 290 (both), 291, 296, 297 (bottom), 298 (bottom), 301 (both), 302, 304-305 (top), 306, 310-311 (bottom), 312 (right), 313, 314-315, 318-319, 320 (top), 321 (bottom), 330-331, 342 (both), 343(right), 344 (right), 346 (left), 350 (both), 351, 352 (right), 353, 356 (bottom), 368 (right), 370, 372, 373, 374 (left), 379 (top), 386 (left), 387 (right), 389 (left), 399 (middle & right), 400 (both), 401 (bottom), 402-403, 404, 405 (both), 418, 420 (left), 422, 423, 450-451 (both), 458-459, 463, 468; Joshua McClure: 234, 326, 327 (both); Juha Ruokangas: 358, 359; Library of Congress: 242; Manzer Guitars: 471 (top), 496, 497, 498 (photo by Nigel Dickson), 499; Martin Guitar: 32 (both), 61, 417 (both), 478, 479, 480 (both), 484 (both), 485, 488-489, 494-495; Museum für Musikinstrumente, University of Leipzig: 255; Guitar Center (photos by Olivier Pojzman): 9, 12-13, 37 (right), 41, 53 (all), 78, 79, 81, 84 (right), 105, 118 (right), 125, 175, 176-177, 182-183 (17th from left); 209, 214-215, 218-219, 224-225, 295 (right), 322 (both), 324, 325 (2nd from right), 335, 336, 360 (right), 361 (right), 362 (left), 363 (both), 364, 365 (top), 367 (both), 371 (both), 376 (left), 378 (right), 379 (bottom), 380 (all), 381, 388 (left), 396 (left), 397 (both), 398 (right), 407, 408, 409, 412 (bottom), 413, 417 (right), 424 (right), 425 (all); Parker Guitars: 439, 506, 507 (all), 508-509; RetroFret: 80, 230-231; Santa Cruz Guitar Company: 436, 444-445, 446, 447, 476, 477; Scott Peterson: Cover, 412 (bottom), 434-435, 438, 440, 441, 442 (both), 443 (both), 448 (both), 449, 452, 453 (all), 456, 457 (top), 460 (both), 461 (all), 462 (both), 471 (bottom), 486 (left), 503 (both); SharonIsbin.com: 35, 472; Tamara Codor: 469; The Ashmolean Museum of Art and Archeology: 240, 252; The Guitar Salon: 5, 233, 250, 262, 263, 274, 276, 289 (both), 464-465; Thomas Brummett: iv, 17, 20, 23, 27, 33, 34, 36 (both), 37 (left & middle), 38, 42, 43 (middle), 54 (left & middle), 64 (right), 66 (left & right), 67, 70 (left), 82 (bottom), 112, 119 (left), 144-145, 182-183 (3rd & 6th from left); 188-189, 194-195, 292, 293 (both); Traugott Guitars: i, 486 (right), 487; Ulrich Teuffel: 510, 511 (both); William Laskin: 466 (left), 467 (all); Youngblood Photography: vi, 426, 437, 501 (both), 500, 502; Zavaleta's La Casa de Guitarras: 286.

David Schiller is an author of eclectic interests whose books include *The Little Zen Companion, All-American Carioke* and *The Runaway Beard*. He dabbled in the guitar as a teenager and then returned to it decades later as a passionate amateur and eternal beginner. His collection is modest— a Gibson L-00, a '62 Reissue Fender Stratocaster, and a stunning Santa Cruz H-13, a guitar far beyond his ability to play as it deserves. He lives with his family in Montclair, New Jersey, and his website is www.davidschiller.com.